CASH
How to achieve more
from a fixed income

CASHWISE

How to achieve more
from a fixed income

FRANK BIRKIN

Kogan
Page

First published in Great Britain
in 1987 by Kogan Page Limited,
120 Pentonville Road, London N1 9JN

British Library Cataloguing in Publication Data

Birkin, Frank
  Cashwise: how to achieve more from a
  fixed income.
  1. Finance, Personal
  I. Title
  332.024   HG179

  ISBN 1-85091-350-1

Printed and bound in Great Britain
by Biddles Ltd, Guildford

Contents

Introduction

Cashwise is the way to effective personal and household cash control and planning. Busy people who use this book will make the most of their income and may discover that financial health removes a measure of individual stress and uncertainty.

Tried and tested business cash control techniques, pertinent examples and concise information are presented free of jargon for non-financial readers. The straightforward Cashwise income and expenditure control system is designed to provide maximum benefits for minimum outlay of time—practical analysis and 'shoe-box' filing tailored to individual requirements.

Expense reduction without discomfort is illustrated by select case histories and a comprehensive guide to saving ideas.

Cash flow forecasting develops logically and easily from the basic system. Domestic budget preparation and operation is explained with an emphasis on what to do when events do not run as planned.

Longer-term financial planning accommodates a variety of situations ranging from cash crisis recovery to investments. Select reference information is given for the financial planner.

Young families are provided with a chapter dedicated to their particular cash problems. The self-employed also have their own chapter in which the Cashwise control system is readily adapted to business use.

Additional control and presentation techniques—including a no-nonsense bank statement reconciliation—make a fittingly practical conclusion.

Chapter 1
Sound Foundations

INTRODUCTION

Doctors in ancient China would not treat people who were already ill. This may seem inconceivable in our sophisticated society but those doctors took the view that if someone became ill, it was just too late to do anything about it.

They were more interested in maintaining health rather than curing the sick, an attitude which is expressed in the saying 'There is no point in closing the gate after the horse has bolted.'

Preventive medicine is beginning to receive more attention today. By eating the right foods, taking regular exercise and following a healthy lifestyle, many people hope to avoid illness; in fact, to do just what the doctors of ancient China recommended.

And so too with our money. If you run your financial life along sound, basic and healthy principles, your wallet or purse will never get sick! Here you will find outlined some of the sound foundations which should lead to financial health.

If you have money problems at the moment, or have ever experienced them, you will know that bank managers behave very much like those Chinese doctors. When you enter a bank with a healthy account, all the bank's services are at your disposal. Go into the same bank with a money problem, however, and the manager will be very sceptical; perhaps he will be unable to help at all.

The truth is that loans and overdrafts are not there to cure a financial problem; they are available only to those who can exhibit security and who have the means to make the repayments.

So a little attention paid to the habits of your financial life will keep your cash flow flowing, your savings growing and help to make your dreams come true.

9

BANKING

Banks are efficient, reliable and provide their basic services for little or no charge. The high street banks, the National Girobank (available at post offices) and an increasing number of building societies are all competing for custom. They will provide regular, tidy statements of income and expenditure, pay bills on your behalf and readily introduce you to a wide range of services all designed to make life easier.

Yet jam jars, shoe boxes, tins and so on, are still used by many people as the basis of their cash control. Naive reasons are trotted out to defend their positions:

'I don't like others handling my money.'

'Banks wouldn't be bothered about my little bit of money.'

'I'm not letting anyone see how much I earn.'

Although this may sound more like an advertisement for a bank rather than a professional guide, it is true to say that banks are interested in anyone with any money at all and their services are confidential—you would be, after all, only one customer among thousands.

You are recommended to make use of banking services if it is possible. With a few pounds to open an account and sómeone willing to stand as a reference, the vast and efficient world of banking is available to you. A child, for example, may open a supersaver's deposit account at Barclays for only £1. There are many ways for a bank to assist in maintaining financial health.

All accounts provide statements which are usually available monthly or on demand. From such statements income and expenditure are easily measured—providing possibly the first glimpse of your own cash flow.

Regular payments from a current or cheque account will be made automatically by means of the 'standing order' or 'direct debit'. No more trips to town, the post office or various showrooms to pay the mortgage, rent, HP, rates, loan, energy, or store accounts. Yet the system is entirely within your control—you tell the bank the date of payments, the payee and the amounts to be paid. A direct debit differs from a standing order in that the actual amount to be paid is not specified. The bank, effectively, is authorised by the customer to pay the billing authority whatever is required. This is useful for paying amounts which tend to vary, such as index-related insurance premiums, some subscriptions, mortgage repayments and rates. The actual amount paid by direct debit will appear on a statement from the billing authority and also on the bank statement.

A cheque book provides a secure alternative to cash for shopping. A stolen wallet or purse with plenty of money in it is a thief's dream. A purloined cheque book—especially when stolen with a cheque authorisation card—may also be used by a thief, but simple protection is available. In general, provided that the bank is informed of the loss without delay, no liability is passed on to the customer.

There are too many banking services on offer—some of which are very specialised—for a complete survey in a book concerned with personal finances, but a summary of these services is given in Appendix 1.

As with so many things, there are advantages and disadvantages. Direct debits, for example, can get out of hand. Chosen wisely, however, banking services can do cash lives a power of good!

OTHER MONEY

In this mechanised age, many money transactions may be made without cash ever changing hands. Huge sums can be transferred from one account to another by means of a simple electronic impulse.

Credit cards, bankers' cards and cheque books mean that one can travel to town, complete a full day's shopping, eat out, perhaps see a show and travel home again without using any 'readies' at all. Electronic shopping trips undertaken in one's own living room may soon be generally possible if we follow the example of the USA.

When this 'other money' is used as an alternative to cash there is no accompanying danger. These methods are, in fact, safer from thieves if the conditions of use are closely followed.

But there are two traps to watch out for:

1. *Having too many different sources of 'other money'.* This could result in being overwhelmed by monthly statements and demands for payment.

   To keep 'other money' under control, it is wise to be restricted and make do with a cheque book and one of the more widely accepted credit cards such as Access or Barclaycard.

2. *Failing to pay the sums due on time* and thereby incurring high interest charges. Most of the 'other money' schemes give a month or so free credit, but if more time than this is used, you may end by paying more than you need in interest.

These are usually expensive forms of credit; it is best to make sure that interest is not charged to your account by paying the statements when due.

BIG BILL

Getting into sound financial order is easiest with a regular income and payments which do not vary greatly in size.

After a few months' application of Cashwise, the amounts of regular expenditure can quickly be calculated. Such payments follow a set pattern which can make planning easy. The nightmare of a cash crisis is often triggered by the untimely arrival of a big bill such as gas, electricity, rates, telephone, car maintenance, income tax demand, yet there is much that can be done to alleviate such an emergency.

Proper insurance can provide protection in the case of a car crash, burst pipes, fire or breakages. Insurance services are dealt with in Chapter 9, *Financially Yours*.

Less dramatic but often very inconvenient problems may arise when domestic appliances fail. If the washing machine, TV, dish washer, vacuum cleaner, tumble-drier and so on break down, their services are soon missed. If you cannot repair it yourself, a relatively large amount may have to be paid to a qualified engineer to do the job.

Extensions of guarantees are offered on many new domestic appliances to cover up to five or six years of use. These are well worth taking up as their cost could be recouped by the savings made on a single breakdown. Service contracts to cover, for example, central heating maintenance are also advisable.

There are many other sources of the disruptive bill—holidays, Christmas time, new furniture or appliances, clothes for the new season—they all occur from time to time.

Cash for such items will probably not be available from the day-to-day running of your finances. Something special needs to be done. The big bill may be tackled in one of two ways:

Savings

If it can be managed, saving for a particular purchase is a financially healthy way of tackling this eventuality. Savings accounts that will earn interest can be opened at a number of places: your bank, the post office, a building society—each has specific advantages. Arrange to transfer a sum each month into the account.

If you have the money available you can shop around and take advantage of special offers, sales and discounts. Money put aside represents security. If a major unforeseen event occurs, there is something on which to fall back.

In recent years easily available credit schemes have tempted increasing numbers of people to become over-committed with inevitable financial crises resulting. If, on the other hand, you buy from savings, it follows that you live within your means.

Credit

Used wisely and frugally loan finance can be the best solution to some problems. My sister-in-law is accustomed to going to work on an old motor bike. Should the bike break down, she would have no other way of getting to work. She and her husband have been in the same jobs for many years and their respective companies are doing well — there is no threat of short-time or redundancies. They have no children. Here a new motor bike, paid for by loan finance, would seem the best thing to do. She could make the repayments easily enough out of her wages. However, should their circumstances change. For instance, should they think of starting a family, my sister-in-law would in due course have to give up her job, temporarily at least and more money would have to be paid on various purchases, so a loan repayment would then not be the best thing.

Taking out too much credit will restrict future options. Even in times of inflation, when the pressure is on to buy before the price goes up, rates of interest will add a lot to the cost of the item. Money lenders are, after all, in business — and, judging by the number of advertisements for loans, a very profitable business at that!

Even interest-free credit will cost more than a cash sale. Discounts, special offers and the ability to shop around are lost.

Credit is not necessary if you have the money. If you do not, credit can become a dangerous trap.

Various forms of credit and loan finance are discussed in Chapter 9.

BILL SPREADER

Payment by instalments

Another way to smooth out cash flow is to pay certain regular bills piecemeal. For example, both British Gas and the Electricity Board operate bill-spreading schemes to help customers cope with their bills, particularly heavy in the winter period.

The schemes come in several forms:

1. *A regular payments scheme* operates so that the cost of a whole year's energy supply can be spread over a span of 10 or 12 months' equal amounts. The sizes of the payments are calculated so that, in total, they cover the likely annual bill.
2. *A 'pay-as-you-go' scheme* permits payments in advance towards the next bill to be made as and when you like. The payments can be any size and may be paid at your local gas or electricity showroom.
3. *Savings stamps* are available to offset these bills and may be purchased in the showrooms and at certain post offices. These are payments also made in advance.
4. *Prepayment meters* installed in the home enable you to pay for gas and electricity as and when consumed. Using this method no large bill will accumulate but a steady supply of coins is required.

   There is, however, a small additional cost for meters.

Local showrooms will have details of the schemes available in the area. Another bill-spreader scheme is to buy special stamps from the post office as a way of saving for your television licence.

Note that those methods which take payments in advance amount to the customers giving credit to the supplier. You will not, however, be given interest for making them the loan! A more attractive alternative would be to accumulate the money in a savings account which does pay interest.

Arrangements can usually be made to pay the local authority rates and water service bills biannually, quarterly or over a ten-month period. This is well worth doing since the payments are made in arrears. Details of these schemes should be provided with the rates demand—if not, they can be obtained at local council information offices. The address and telephone numbers can be found in the telephone directory.

Shop accounts

Many large department stores operate customer accounts by which the cost of purchases may be postponed or spread. Three such schemes are:

1. *Monthly account*

   This is the basic type of account with a store which will present a bill each month for purchases made. Thus shopping can be done without cash, cheque book or credit card. You will simply need your account card. Failure to pay the monthly statement, however, will result in interest being added to your account and, possibly, demand notes.

2. *Option account*

   The option account is similar to the monthly one, except that settlement is not expected each time you receive the statement. Time to pay is allowed but interest will be charged.

3. *Budget account*

   This is a more specialised account into which an agreed amount is paid each month. Purchases up to a certain fixed figure are permitted. The total figure is calculated as a multiple of the monthly payments made.

   For example, if £10 a month is paid into the account and the store allows purchases up to 24 times the monthly payment, then you may buy on credit up to £240-worth of goods. But interest will be charged on any unpaid balances in this account.

If you habitually shop at one of two stores such shop accounts may be suitable. They will, however, limit the possibility of shopping around and can work out expensive if interest, usually at a high rate, has to be paid.

Stamp saving schemes are available for TV licences, Christmas Clubs and other expenses but it should be remembered that these schemes take money in advance and do not give interest. Again, a savings account at a bank or building society makes better financial sense.

The same point should be borne in mind for any 'bill spreader' scheme that requires payments in advance without offering interest.

Finally, there is the option of bringing many of these bill spreading schemes under one roof. A budget account available at most banks will permit all bills to be paid as and when they arise.

A little planning is required. An estimate of the total amount to be paid out of your budget account in one year should be made and the bank informed. They will then divide this by 12 to obtain the size of the monthly repayment.

For example, looking through last year's bills you may find the total for gas, electricity, garage, insurance, holidays and odd major purchases was £3420. Add on some for Christmas and inflation at, say, 7 per cent to give a grand total of approximately £4000.

This is the total you expect to pay out of your budget account. Dividing £4000 by 12 gives £333, the amount to be paid into the budget account each month—usually by standing order from a current account.

Once this system is established, payments can be made from the budget account when necessary even if the account becomes overdrawn. But interest will be charged on the overdrawn amounts.

This may be the way to spread the cost of most of your large bills by one straightforward scheme. But there is no point in using such an account for those bills which may be spread free of charge anyway, such as the rates.

RECORDS

While on the subject of building sound foundations into personal and home finances, the keeping of adequate records must be mentioned. Since most of these will probably be financial or finance related, it would seem good sense to keep all such documentation together.

For a typical household this type of record would include the following classifications:

Banking
Building society
Car expenses
Household accounts
House repairs
Income tax
Insurances
Investments
Legal
Medical
Miscellaneous
Rates.

Important documents such as insurance policies, share certificates, wills, deeds and the like are best kept in a secure safe deposit away from the house.

Finally, a word for computer addicts. Cashwise is a system which embraces data collection, data analysis, information presentation and control action. Data analysis and information presentation are the most suitable of these stages for tackling by a computer.

The basic Cashwise system is presented in this book but a major feature lies in its flexibility. After a few months of using Cashwise, the system becomes tailor-made—specifically designed for each individual user.

If you wish to bring a computer into the system, the manual Cashwise should be operated for several months before effecting a transfer.

Chapter 2
Expenses Control

INTRODUCTION

In any business possibly the most important figure is sales value. Then comes sales cost. It is only when this figure is known that profit—or loss—may be calculated.

It should not come as a surprise to learn that considerable time and money are expended to find out the cost of a product or service. This knowledge forms the basis of cost control. First you have to ask 'How much time?', 'How much material?' and 'How many machine hours?'.

Questions such as 'Just where is the money going?', 'How can we spend less?' become more important for the business person if sales income is static, and they are just as important for people whose income is pretty well fixed.

Nowadays maintaining and buying a house, running a car, obtaining all those domestic appliances and keeping a family fed, clothed and entertained can be as complicated as running a small business.

The expense control analysis of Cashwise will make valuable information readily available. The system grows to satisfy particular requirements—when the basics have been operated for two or three months, you will be able to tune in as you wish.

For the sake of an hour or so each month, you will know the facts about your personal and household expenses and have the kind of information which enables you to plan and make considerable savings, which points the right way to decide and thus save months or years of worry.

CASHWISE HQ

The expense control procedures of Cashwise have been devised for simplicity and ease of operation. They have to be well organised but

19

this can be done at minimum expense. Just five simple items are needed:

1. One dozen 9 x 6 inch manilla envelopes
2. Pad of lined notepaper—A4 size (11¾ x 8¼ inches)
3. Box of paper clips
4. Pencil
5. Container for the envelopes and other items (a drawer or small box would do).

Cashwise requires a minimum of calculations which are easily done, but you may find a pocket calculator helpful.

BASICS

To understand and reduce expenditure, there are two questions to answer:

1. How much do you spend?
2. Where do you spend it?

Whenever you spend money you get a receipt. It is sensible, since a receipt is proof of purchase if you wish to return goods or raise a query.

It would be too time-consuming to attempt to collect and analyse every single receipt that passes through your hands, but there are ways to streamline the procedures. A decision is required about the smallest value of receipt to be saved. A 30p bus ticket, 80p for a bag of sweets, £1-worth of stamps are not very significant. A cut-off point is required.

The rate of cut-off is naturally determined by your level of affluence. If you happen to be a well-paid company director you will probably not think twice about a costly night out but a state pensioner may be bothered about the cost of a newspaper, for example. That cut-off best suited to your circumstances may not be apparent until Cashwise has been operated for a few months and you have observed the frequency and size of your receipts. Suppose we take a cut-off point of £10.

The cost of daily newspapers, weekly magazines, milk, bread and any other items which are delivered regularly may not amount to much individually but can be significant over a month.

The way to account for these small value, regular items is *either* to pay for them on a monthly account (easily done for most deliveries), *or* estimate their monthly cost and use this figure. For example, every day you buy a newspaper on the way to work. Your spouse does the same. So reckoning that the newspapers cost about 50p each working day and say £2 on Sundays, then estimate: 50p for six days plus £2 for Sunday, giving £5 a week or £20 a month.

To cover the sundry small items paid from the change in your pocket, a 'Personal Allowance' may be made. Estimate the total of a person's odd expenditure for each month, and record this figure on a sheet in the current month envelope. Just how much personal allowance is given and what it is intended to cover is up to you.

The same principle may be applied to purchases of food, other household and personal consumables. Buying them from an allowance enables control to be exercised over them while avoiding the time-consuming volumes of receipts.

If you pay by cheque, credit card, store account or other credit facility, there will be another set of records as a reminder of purchases and the cheque stubs, credit payment vouchers or paying-in book will provide the specific information required. Ensure that sufficient description is always provided of the items purchased for your future reference.

All receipts, credit vouchers, mail-order slips, tradesmen's bills and your own notes and estimates may then be stored in the current month's envelope. The receipts and other records of purchase represent the 'source documents' for Cashwise's expense control.

And so, one way or another, the envelope will grow fatter and fatter each month as your expense records accumulate. At the end of each calendar month, the envelope is emptied. It may then be used again.

Place the receipts from the previous month into the Cashwise HQ. Be careful that the receipts are grouped together according to their dates and keep each month separate.

SORT OUT

After the first complete month of operating Cashwise's expense control system, there will be a collection of receipts sitting in HQ. You probably have a rough idea of their total from a bank statement or the fact that all your wages and salaries have been spent!

It is necessary to know about your expenditure patterns. Some time each month find a spare hour to tackle the sorting out stage of the 'data analysis' exercise. To extract the information needed categorise the receipts by sorting them into several piles, totalling each one.

Receipt categories that particularly relate to what is actually happening would be based on:

—the kind of item or service being purchased;
—the place or person from which the purchase was made.

If the receipts have to be categorised by the type of purchase only, the slips of paper would be sorted into piles like these:

Groceries
Household consumables
Personal consumables
Garage
Gas
Electricity
Clothing
Medical
Drinks
Telephone
Entertainment

Totalling your expenditure by each of these categories will probably bring a few surprises. Not only may large, potential savings become apparent on the more expensive items but the small regular purchases may be shown to have significant totals over a month. Minor, painless changes in habit will probably save you pounds and pounds.

SHOPPER'S WORLD

Having receipts sorted according to the type of item or service purchased is the most useful classification. This is not so easily achieved.

The problem lies in the fact that many different types of item may be bought in a single store—and all tallied on the same receipt. If you shop once a week at a hypermarket you will know what is meant.

So as to relate receipt categories ever closer to what is actually happening in your life, the places where items or services are obtained must also be considered. When you come to total up, all the items purchased in one shop will usually be on one single receipt. The way to deal with such receipts is to tackle them in three stages:

1. Sort them according to place of purchase.
2. Work out totals for each category of item on the actual receipt and write the figures down on the slip.

3. Using these item totals, add through the pile to obtain the full total for the relevant store.

On the day of purchase, or before you forget all about it, identify the expensive items if necessary. Then put the receipt in the current month envelope.

Here is a sample receipt:

XYZ Supermarket   11/4/8X

5.67
2.35
0.63
20.95
1.23
0.10
0.86
21.00
1.00
0.40
0.10
54.29

Note on the receipt that the £20.95 was for drinks and the £21.00 for clothing. The other items were a mixture of groceries and general household consumables. If you can remember the approximate breakdown of the other items, make a note of that on the slip as well. If not, there is only £12.34 remaining so do not bother any more about that.

And so for this receipt, you would have a rough description and value of the items as follows:

Drinks	£20.95
Clothing	£21.00
Groceries	£6.00
Consumables	£6.34

Bear in mind that the cut-off level will screen off the vast number of purchases anyway; they will be accounted for in the allowances.

The job of analysis is nearing completion. A *Checklist of expenditure items* is provided here as a guide.

Checklist of expenditure items

Alimony
Baby
Birthdays
Business expenses
  books
  entertaining
  tools
  travel
Car
  garage
  insurance
  licence
  loan
  petrol
  repairs
  road fund
Children
  baby-sitter
  playgroup
  pocket money
Christmas
Deeds of covenant
Donations and gifts
Education
  music lessons
  school fees
  school meals
  uniform
  university fees
Fares
  bus
  rail cards
  season ticket
  taxis
  train
  tube
Food
  dairy produce

   fish
   freezer purchases
   fruit
   groceries
   meat
   poultry
   vegetables
Garden
Hire purchase
Hobbies
   photography
   stereo system
   other
Holidays
   annual
   weekends
House or flat
   furnishings
   insurance
   maintenance
      cleaning supplies
      consumables
      daily help
      decoration
      DIY
      insulation
      modification
      repairs
      service charges (for flat)
   power
      gas
      electricity
   purchase
   rates
   rents
Income tax
Life assurance
Loans
Medical
   BUPA
   dentist

hospital
medicines
optician
Milkman
Mortgage
Motorbike
Newspapers, magazines
Pension schemes
Personal
  clothes
  cosmetics
  dry cleaning
  hairdresser
  laundry
Personal allowances
Pets
  food
  kennelling
  vet
Professional fees
  accountant
  solicitor
Recreation
  cigarettes
  drinks
  entertaining
  sport
  tickets (concerts, music, theatres)
Services (see Professional fees)
Subscriptions
  clubs
  membership
  societies
  union
Telephone
TV
  licence
  rental
Video
Wedding(s)

AS MUCH AS THAT?

At this stage, a pile of sorted receipts, credit vouchers, cheque book stubs and the like, will be available. In the conglomeration of paper lies the story of your expenditure for the month. If you have only a few receipts, enter the figures on to the Cashwise statement on page 29.

If there are many receipts or they are complicated in some way, you may like to bring the data into a higher degree of order before entering the figures on the statement. Simply list them on a sheet of A4 paper.

Example

	April 198X				
	XYZ Supermarket	Bijou Stores	A1 Chemist	Bob's Garage	Totals £
Groceries	40	57	—	—	97
Consumables	23	18	—	—	41
Petrol	—	—	—	47	47
Clothes	—	27	—	—	27
Drinks	18	16	—	—	34
Medical	11	—	14	—	25
					271

Either from a sheet of this sort or direct from receipts or allowances, the basic expenditure information for the Cashwise statement becomes available.

EXPENSE STATEMENT

The Cashwise statement presents a detailed expense analysis for each month. As months pass, Cashwise will provide a steady stream of accurate and useful information.

This statement provides lines for the expense categories in use, and columns for each month. Each statement takes up to six months' figures as the expenditure pattern will be more noticeable only after three or four months' figures have been entered—and the six-month point provides a convenient review period.

Complete the Cashwise statement with your own figures using the example as a guide. You can copy the blank Cashwise statement on pages 30-31.

It may be more convenient if the statement falls in line with the calendar year with one statement for the six months January to June, and another for July to December.

Cashwise Statement

Year: 1987

Half Year: 1st/2nd

Month actual/budget	Jan a	Jan b	Feb a	Feb b	Mar a	Mar b	Apr a	Apr b	May a	May b	Jun a	Jun b	Total a	Total b
Income														
Sub-total (1)														
Expenditure														
Groceries etc	108		130		96									
Butcher	19		15		14									
Milk/eggs	24		21		24									
School meals	20		24		24									
Drinks	18		11		27									
Entertaining	37		22		34									
Clothes	29		1		149									
Newsagents	14		16		14									
My allowance	80		80		80									
Joan's allowance	25		25		25									

Expenditure (cont.)				
Bus fares	12		17	17
Electricity	-		242	-
Gas	-		-	191
Mortgage	212		212	212
Life assurance	28		28	28
Rates - general	65		65	-
- water	-		-	71
Telephone	-		-	58
Consumables	11		14	9
Petrol and Oil	26		39	27
Sundries - TV repair	19		-	-
- garage	-		98	-
- carpet	-		410	-
- car insur.	-		-	142
Sub-total (2)	747		1529	1241
Cash in Hand				
Opening Balance				
Movement (1-2)				
Closing Balance				

Statement completed for expenditure only.

Cashwise Statement

Year: Half Year: 1st/2nd

Month actual/budget	a	b	a	b	a	b	a	b	a	b	a	b	a	b	Total a	b
Income																
Sub-total (1)																
Expenditure																

Expenditure (cont.)																									
Sub-total (2)																									
Cash in Hand																									
Opening Balance																									
Movement (1-2)																									
Closing Balance																									

This brings an easily remembered sequence to the statements and makes inter-year comparisons easier.

Your first Cashwise statement will probably not cover a full six-month period. Beginning in October, for example, the first statement would cover October, November and December, and the next would be in line with the calendar year, covering January to June.

An alternative would be to have the statements coinciding with the tax year which runs approximately from April to March.

All the little chores are now complete. Time to be reminded that Cashwise is going to save you money. Develop an eye for watching the figures and understand just what they represent. Pay attention to the higher value items at first since this is where the greatest savings are to be made.

The receipts, vouchers, statements and so on are of no more immediate use. Some of the receipts may be required in the future for guarantee claims or returning defective goods. They all may have a back-up role to play in support of the Cashwise statement.

Those you wish to save may be stored conveniently in a manilla envelope in the Cashwise HQ.

Chapter 3
Income

Income for the majority of people comes from one, two, or at the most three regular sources. The income block on the Cashwise statement is, therefore, correspondingly smaller. For most households, the types of income to be included on the statement include:

Husband's wage or salary
Wife's wage or salary
Business earnings
Freelance earnings
Child benefits
Housekeeping contribution from a working offspring
Interest
Dividends
Rents
Pensions
DHSS benefits.

It may be argued, quite rightly, that certain incomes should be kept separate from this general pool. A wife may wish to hang on to her salary, to keep child benefit specifically for the children, or anyone in the family may prefer to keep their own freelance earnings. This is a matter for discussion—and agreement.

When entering salaries or wages, overtime earnings, bonuses and commission must all be included. The figure required is the actual cash received into the household.

So, likewise, enter the income figures net of all deductions such as tax, National Insurance, pension contributions and so on. The Cashwise statement will then be complete and will give the actual cash flow over each monthly period.

A cash-in-hand figure may be calculated at each month end. The

Cashwise Statement

Year: 1987

Half Year: 1st/2nd

Month actual/budget	Jan a	Jan b	Feb a	Feb b	Mar a	Mar b	Apr a	Apr b	May a	May b	Jun a	Jun b	Total a	Total b
Income														
My salary	718		756		810									
Joan's salary	126		126		125									
Freelance	59		1		1									
Dividends	1		93		1									
Interest	1		26		1									
Sale of car	1		1		1620									
Sub-total (1)	963		1001		2555									
Expenditure														

Expenditure (cont.)											
Sub-total (2)											
Cash in Hand											
Opening Balance											
Movement (1-2)											
Closing Balance											

Statement completed for income only.

Year: 1987

Cashwise Statement

Half Year: 1st/2nd

Month actual/budget	Jan a	b	Feb a	b	Mar a	b	Apr a	b	May a	b	Jun a	b	Total a	b
Income														
My salary	778		756		810									
Joan's salary	126		126		125									
Dividends	–		93		–									
Sale of car	–		–		1620									
Interest	–		26		1									
Freelance	59		1		1									
Sub-total (1)	963		1001		2555									
Expenditure														
Groceries etc	108		130		96									
Butcher	19		15		14									
Milk/eggs	24		21		24									
School Meals	20		24		24									
Drinks	18		11		27									
Entertaining	37		22		34									
Clothes	29		–		149									
Newsagents	14		16		14									
My allowance	80		80		80									
Joan's allowance	25		25		25									

Expenditure (cont.)					
Bus fares	12	17	17		
Electricity	-	242	-		
Gas	-	-	191		
Mortgage	212	212	212		
Life assurance	28	28	28		
Rates - general	65	65	-		
~ water	-	-	71		
Telephone	-	-	58		
Consumables	11	14	9		
Petrol and Oil	26	39	27		
Sundries - TV repair	19	-	-		
- carpet	-	470	-		
- garage	-	98	-		
- car insur.	-	-	142		
Sub-total (2)	747	1529	1242		
Cash in Hand					
Opening Balance	(67)	149	(379)		
Movement (1-2)	216	(528)	1313		
Closing Balance	149	(379)	934		

Statement completed for actual income and expenditure only.

cash-in-hand balance at the end of the previous month becomes the opening cash balance for the current month.

Example

		£
	Last month's closing balance	<u>419.06</u>
Plus:	Current month's net income	926.17
Less:	Current month's expenses	(1,107.82)
	Current month's closing cash	<u>237.41</u>

The £237.41 should agree approximately with the cash in hand and in the bank. It is very unlikely, however, that an accurate match will occur since, while the income figures may be spot on, the expense statement will not be. There are so many small items of expenditure, so many possibilities for mistakes, that a totally accurate cash flow statement is not available—nor is it necessary.

The Cashwise statement is designed to be a control tool to assist in the management of your money—it is not an account. The additional effort required to make the statement 100 per cent accurate is not justified for the purposes of the vast majority of users.

For those who wish for such accuracy, however, the preparation of an income and expenditure account is dealt with in Chapter 10.

Chapter 4
The Pay-off

INTRODUCTION

The clerical work has been done. At this point, in a company, the financial controller and a director would take over to reap the benefits!

After a month or two, the preparation of the Cashwise statement will be simple and can be completed very quickly. Now is the time to seek out the pay-off for your efforts.

Beginning with the higher value expenses on the statement, select targets to understand and on which to reap savings. A little imagination, a questioning attitude and some thought all play a part here.

At your HQ, with that hour set aside, use the sequences of figures on the statement and the receipts back-up to find out just where the money has gone in those target areas. When you have a good idea of where the money went, ask yourself how you could spend less.

Use the figures to evaluate if worthwhile savings can be made without discomfort. Bear in mind that drastic or uncomfortable changes are not normally required to save considerable sums of money.

Time will be saved if you distinguish the uncontrollable from the controllable expenses. Those costs and payments which are unalterable by you without drastic or major action are uncontrollable. This includes, for example, mortgage repayments, rates, rent, hire purchase payments, loan repayments and insurance premiums. It is true that they can be changed, but that would usually involve major extraordinary effort such as moving house, changing cars, returning HP goods and so on. All feasible, but not very likely on a regular month-to-month basis.

All your expenses are controllable in the longer term, but for the purposes of Cashwise it is best to concentrate on those which yield to easy manipulation. The Cashwise Statement provides the information you require to control and reduce expenditure. Now is the time for decision and action. Here are a few examples selected for their potential wide application and minimum inconvenience. Some of the suggestions might bring benefits to you and your family other than just saving money.

TO AND FRO

Friends of my family, Jennifer and Richard, have two boys and a baby girl, and their house is in the Cheshire countryside. They badly wanted an overseas holiday—they would save for it. Unfortunately their savings would grow for a month or two then virtually disappear on a garage bill, a new TV and other unforeseen demands. Their vacation did not seem to be within their reach.

I suggested that a professional approach and a systematic reappraisal of his expenses might help. Richard began to use Cashwise.

Several shocks were in store for him, but he was appalled by the overall cost of their two cars, one for him to go to work and one for Jennifer who used it mainly for the 6½ mile trip to school. The cars were old and required almost weekly attention: this took large slices out of his spare time, as well as out of his pocket.

They liked their house and did not wish to move. No other schools lay any closer and there was no convenient bus. The cost of those cars was not to be ignored and Jennifer took up the problem when she saw the Cashwise figures. They had estimated the total cost of the second car to be around £45 to £50 per month. If they could save that—£600 a year—that overseas holiday was theirs.

Jennifer reckoned that if Richard could take the boys to school—which would mean that he would be slightly late for work—and if she could find someone to bring the boys back from school, the second car could go. She would use the bus to go shopping.

At school Jennifer put the word around that she was trying to establish a school run. A lady in a similar situation was interested and they lived in the same area.

Richard took the boys to school, the new-found friend brought them back, and Jennifer often got a lift to the shops anyway. The second car went.

They managed their holiday and plan to repeat it.

CLEAN UP

Another family friend decided to tackle the cost of cleaning supplies—everything she bought to keep her house and her family clean.

From several months of Cashwise, she could see the typical cost of all these cleaning items. Then she decided to have a blitz—to re-think everything from how much soap powder she used to how often she cleaned the bath.

No sacrifices on cleanliness were to be made. Care, close examination of old habits and experimentation were to bring in the economies. All the family was expected to help in this.

She found that many manufacturers were too generous with their recommended measures. From her experiments, she found that sufficient cleaning power could be obtained from two-thirds or one-half of the recommended quantity. Care with the little things like shaving foam and toothpaste meant that they could be made to last half as long again. The children were not to use soap—and hot water—when playing at washing their toys.

After a few weeks of conscious scrutiny and economies, she found that she and her family had a new set of habits—just as easy and unthinking to follow as the old set, but the new ones saved money.

Having completed her blitz and passed two months under the new regime, she re-assessed the cleaning costs on the Cashwise statement.

'I'm saving over £15 a month,' she told me with enthusiasm. Even if her estimate was over-generous, she could well be saving over £120 a year—this year and next year, and the one after that.

WHAT, NO MEAT!

An area for savings was impressed on my family when we returned from Kenya to live in England. This is concerned with the traditional English dinner. My wife and I are omnivorous and had never tasted even one nut cutlet before our return. We were, therefore, a little apprehensive when our new neighbours invited us around to dinner and told us that they were vegetarian. We were surprised to find that we liked the vegetarian curry and accompaniments that they served up. We went on to make and enjoy our own vegetarian food: tabboulehs, ratatatouille, croquettes, curries, sauces and the like.

Now we savour a far greater range of dishes and enjoy a weekly mixture of vegetarian and meat meals. This, we are told, is better for our health—I do not know too much about that but I do enjoy those tasty vegetarian dishes.

So, if you wish to find a whole new range of dishes to please your family, improve their health and still make significant savings—try a few vegetarian meals.

Check out the meat costs on your Cashwise statement. Aim to halve this bill or more. You may not only feel better, but be that much richer.

CENTRAL HEATING

One of the most satisfying rewards of Cashwise is to be able to see a substantial saving being made as a direct result of your own research. Our local garage manager is a very busy man, with a good salary, but he is a little profligate concerning his personal and household expenses. His wife took it upon herself to run the house as efficiently as he ran the business. Cashwise is invaluable to her.

Her proudest achievement was in controlling the gas central heating system of their four-bedroomed, detached house. Her husband used to keep the house quite warm all day long for the family. She turned the thermostat down, turned off radiators in unused rooms, set the timers precisely, kept doors closed and issued winter woollies as regulation wear about the house. She found she had made a substantial saving on the heavy winter quarter's bill.

PETS

I once had an elderly relative who was keeping herself, a dog and three cats on a pension. With her limited income, she was paying out a relatively large sum on proprietary pet foods. It was a case of spoilt animals eating only the best, and over-eating at that.

The animals did not really need to cost so much to keep. Table scraps, more filler, and butcher's scraps would have kept them just as healthy as the expensive pet foods. She wouldn't listen to this, however. The pets had to have the best.

You can't win them all!

There are many ways in which Cashwise can help you to take control of your personal finances and save yourself money as well. Cashwise is a tool—it is there if you need it and, with a little skill, a good job can be done with it.

The method, presentation, approach, action and results monitoring are all based on the professional ways of controlling costs used throughout industry. The benefit of all this experience is yours for the taking.

The small amount of work required is soon completed and becomes very easy after one or two months of operation. The information available can be tailored to your individual requirements, by selecting the categories of expenses to be analysed and the level of detail for the analyses.

Be flexible in your approach and do not be afraid of changing the Cashwise statement. Be careful not to make too many changes, however, since this will make historic, year-by-year comparisons and budget preparation more difficult.

In too many lives, money rules. Let Cashwise make sure that you are in control—that the money looks after itself and you reap the benefits.

Chapter 5
Cash Savers

INTRODUCTION

Here is a compilation of ideas, some new, some well tried, based on sound common sense, others requiring technical assistance. They range from heating, shopping, transport to health and leisure. Any of these or all of them, if brought to bear on your way of life, should produce economies and save money.

POWER

These bills will be among the largest you have to pay. In order to decide whether to use gas, electricity or oil, you should get up-to-date information from your local gas or electricity showroom. Efficient systems are vitally important and ways of making them more so are suggested here. Proper insulation will save a lot on heating (see page 49). Using your thermostat sensibly, or in some cases switching off appliances, may be the best way.

Energy cost comparisons

To make a meaningful comparison between the costs of gas versus electricity as used in a home is not possible in general terms. The comparison depends on the appliances used, rates charged and available, type of house, degree of insulation and energy consumption habits.

Cashwise enables you to make the most of whatever fuels are already installed in your home. To assess the economic worth of installing new appliances of a different fuel type (eg a move from electric to gas central heating), any potential savings in fuel costs must be offset against purchase and installation costs. Detailed information and advice necessary for you to compile your own assessment will be available from your local gas and electricity showrooms.

Heating

Turning thermostat controls down by 1 °C could reduce your heating costs by as much as 10 per cent.

Timer controls are essential for central heating systems. The regular patterns of life in many households mean that accurate switching on and off of the heating system is possible. Don't waste money heating the house when you are not there or are tucked up snug in bed.

A seven-day timer control enables different switching sequences to be set up for different days of the week. The Sunday morning lie-in, for example, would mean that the heating could come on an hour or two later than in the week.

Get into the habit of turning the heating down whenever you leave the house for a short period, or off altogether for a longer absence. This could be done at a switch or by turning the thermostat controls down, whichever is more convenient.

Lighting

Use lower wattage bulbs where possible. If you have lampshades that obstruct the passage of light, then think about using clear or open shades. This is a more efficient way of providing as much—or more— light than diffuse shades with powerful bulbs.

Table and floor lighting can be used to deliver economic light where it is needed for evening relaxation. A well positioned, low watt bulb can be all that is required—and far more cosy—in place of the glare of powerful, whole-room lighting.

Fluorescent lights use less electricity than conventional bulbs and give a pleasant light. Although fluorescent strips are generally considered to be only fit for kitchen lighting, there are many different fluorescent light units available for other rooms. There are also fluorescent bulbs which use a fraction of the electricity consumed by tungsten bulbs, yet give the same light.

Dimmer switches are relatively easy to fit in place of normal switches. They provide easy conversion from full room 'activity' lighting to attractive, low-level light using less electricity. Be careful, however, when making economies in the use of lights not to increase the risk of accidents by making stairs and passages too dark. And do not invite burglars by leaving the whole house in darkness when there is no one at home.

Hot water

Hot water is taken for granted in many households. Whether it is heated by gas, electricity or coal, you spend a lot of money to raise those temperatures.

Here's how to make some savings:

(a) If you have a hot-water tank which is not lagged, then do the job (see page 53 on DIY). Lagging jackets come in a range of sizes to fit most common tanks. Measure the height of your tank and buy an 80 mm, or thicker jacket which can be found in any DIY store.

They won't cost much more than £4 to £6 and may be fitted in 30 minutes. The cost of the jacket is quickly recovered by reduced heat loss. Incidentally, make sure that the jacket fits extra snugly around the top of the tank for this is where the greatest heat loss occurs. Once fitted, the jacket carries on saving you money—year in, year out.

And don't forget to lag the pipes too. Suitable pipe sleeves are inexpensive, easily fitted and will protect against freezing in the winter.

(b) Hot water taps that drip represent your money flowing down the drain—fix them!

(c) Never wash with the hot water running straight down the plug-hole. Put the plug in and you will use less hot water.

(d) Showers use far less hot water than a bath—make good use of the shower. If you do not have one, check out the DIY stores for the cheap, easy to install showers-in-the-bathtub. You could improve your home and reduce the running costs.

(e) Check the hot-water tank thermostat to see that you are not overheating the water. The recommended maximum settings are given below but you may prefer cooler water—especially if there are young children in the house.

For normal water—up to 70°C/160°F
For hard water—up to 60°C/140°F
For soft water—up to 80°C/180°F

Even a setting just a few degrees lower will save you significant sums over the years.

(f) If the hot water heating unit is separate from your central heating, switch it on and off as required. Do not leave it on day and night. A time switch is required for this job. They are easy to fit and not expensive.

(g) If you have children, make sure they are aware that hot water costs money and should be used carefully; that they should use cold water whenever possible.

(h) When using a kettle, heat up only the amount of water required for immediate use. Any extra water in the kettle will take that much longer to heat up and will quickly lose that heat too.

Remember, however, that the kettle's immersion element must always be covered by water before switching on. Jug kettles can be more economical in this respect than conventional designs.

Laundry

To run a home laundry cost-effectively, save up the washing for full loads and run the washing machine and tumble drier at manufacturer's recommended full capacity. Be careful not to exceed the given capacity since this may damage the machine.

Read the washing and ironing instructions on clothing carefully. Not all garments require a hot wash and many require only a cool iron, or you can buy non-iron clothes if preferred.

Finally do not forget nature. If the sun is shining or the wind blowing for a good drying day, put the washing out on the line.

Fridges and freezers

Keep these appliances in good working order. Defrost regularly and ensure that door and lid seals fit properly.

Open the fridge door as seldom as possible to limit the loss of cold air. If your upright fridge or freezer is usually only part full, put in a few empty cardboard boxes to fill the spaces and thus limit the amount of cold air available to spill across the kitchen floor. Note that chest freezers lose less heat than upright ones when opened.

Do not put hot food and drink into these appliances. Let all foodstuffs cool to room temperature first.

INSULATION

In cold weather, there is a steady flow of heat from a house day and night. The more energy — and money — spent to raise the temperature indoors, the greater the seepage of heat to the outside world.

From a typical, semi-detached house without insulation, the escaping heat flow is roughly as follows:

	Percentage heat loss
Roof	25
Walls	35
Windows	10
Floors	15
Draughts	15
Total	100

In different types of houses, the area proportions of roof, walls, floor and windows would change and so, of course, would the heat flow percentages.

Much of this heat loss can be prevented with modern insulating materials. There is a need for care when considering an expensive insulation project; if the cost of insulation is high then many years of heating-cost savings would be required merely to recoup your expenses. This remains true even when the value added to the property is considered.

So, unless you intend to stay in the property for many years, some insulation projects require caution, while others are so cheap, so effective in saving energy money that if you have not got them, I recommend that you start work tomorrow.

Loft insulation

A 4-inch layer of a proprietary glass-fibre laid in the loft may save as much as 15 per cent of the annual heating bill. The job is not difficult and may be tackled with confidence by the home handyman. When the glass-fibre has been laid down, water tanks and pipes in the loft space must be lagged since they are at a greater risk of freezing.

If you do not wish to do the job yourself you can get outside help and sometimes government grants are available for this. They may pay for 66 or 90 per cent of the cost—enquire at your local council offices to see if funds are available, and what the conditions are.

Draught elimination

A remarkably easy way of cutting down on heat losses due to draughts is to keep doors closed. Even so, however, the draughts still come. There are several different types of product on the market designed to stop draughts. Most are fitted easily within an hour and are cheap to buy.

Draught-excluding adhesive strips are available for window joints at a cost of a few pounds. Door draughts may be sealed with on-door or threshold sealers. Spend a little time in one of the large DIY super-markets to discover what is available.

Unused flues or chimneys should also be sealed. A ventilation cap must be fitted to the top of the stack and a ventilation grille to the chimney flue or breast. This is to prevent the build-up of condensation.

Remember to provide some ventilation to all rooms where there are coal, gas or oil heaters.

The insulating materials mentioned below may be fitted to your home at a higher order of cost.

Double glazing

Double glazing is estimated to be capable of reducing heat loss by about 12 per cent (note the estimated 15 per cent reduction achieved by loft insulation). Much of the loss to be saved occurs in the evenings and at night—the time when the temperature differential between indoors and outdoors is at its greatest. This is also the time when curtains are drawn and a thick pair of curtains will, in fact, be almost as good a window insulation as double glazing.

Window frames, however, need replacing from time to time. Street noise can spoil an evening's relaxation. There are other reasons for having double glazed windows fitted.

If your frames need to be replaced, replace them with double-glazed frames. But even then bear in mind that double glazing will be most cost effective in those rooms which take most of the heat—living room, dining room and kitchen. The bedrooms, bathrooms and others could take cheaper, conventional frames.

So far the factory-sealed, double-glazed unit has been considered. There are other, cheaper methods of achieving a similar job. They are:

— a second window which may be clipped or hinged on to the existing frames;
— the DIY plastic film which is so easy to fit.

Cavity wall fillings

By having the cavities in the exterior walls filled with a suitable material, savings of over 20 per cent of your heating bill are possible. The job is done by specialist firms and takes a day or two with minimum inconvenience.

The firm to be used must be selected with care. Make sure that the products and methods they use conform with British Standards S617 and S618.

There is an increased risk of dampness after treatment. If your house has a damp problem, get it seen to before having the walls filled.

Cavity wall insulation is well worth having if you are planning to stay in the house a few years.

Floor insulation

This is not a job usually undertaken for its own sake. A suitable time to increase floor insulation is when you re-carpet. Use ample underlay and thick carpets, seal gaps in wooden floors and around skirting boards.

With a new wooden floor, extra insulation can be acquired by fixing a layer of paper-backed glass fibre below the floor boards.

COOKING

Cooking is such a commonplace, routine activity that the cost of the energy used is often overlooked. Electricity Board figures show that an average family of four uses around 20 units of electricity a week.

Gas is cheaper but even so, much energy can be saved by a few sensible habits that take no effort to employ. Here are the cook's saver tips.

1. Try to fill the oven when it is to be used. A complete meal, for example, may include a roast with jacket potatoes, casseroled vegetables and a baked sweet.

2. Keep pans covered with a lid and use only small amounts of water—use enough, however, to ensure that the pans do not boil dry.
3. Slice vegetables thinly whenever possible; they will cook more quickly. Saucepans with several internal compartments will cook a range of foods cheaply. The stir-fry cooking method is very economical and produces excellent results.
4. If you possess small cooking appliances, make good use of them. The following items, for example, will cook more cheaply than an oven or hot plate: pressure cooker, electric toaster, sandwich toaster, slow cooker, microwave, contact grill and multi-purpose cooker.

To save time and creative energy as well as money, cook several sittings of a meal at one go. Freeze that not required on the day. Sauce-based meals are particularly suited to this approach because they may be reheated with ease. Try it with curries, bolognese sauce, casseroles and stews.

SHOPPING

Buy cheap and save money! That is the name of the game, provided quality does not suffer. There are many ways of achieving this objective.

One method is to shop around and visit other stores to see how prices compare. Special offers, seasonal prices, discontinued lines and the 'slightly damaged' basket are worth looking for.

The possibility of substituting a less expensive item for a dearer one is another consideration. When making a substitution the cheaper one may not be inferior in quality. Prices vary between manufacturers and according to the materials used in the product. Some supermarkets produce their own lines, nearly always cheaper than a brand name.

More expensive appliances, for example, may have features not found on the standard model—but would you use those features? Major purchases should always be well researched and one should not be swayed by sales talk or advertising. The consumer's magazine *Which?* is an excellent source of information and should be available at your local library or might be worth a subscription.

Buying in bulk at the home freezer stores will bring the item cost down. Another way to buy in bulk is to form a 'shopping club' among your friends and neighbours. The club buys in bulk and divides the purchases among its members. Savings of up to one-third of your shopping bill may be possible. The *Bulk Buy Book* from the National Consumer Council at 18 Queen Anne's Gate, London SW1H 9AA shows you how to do all this.

Clothing can be expensive. Savings can be achieved by making some clothes at home. If you have no experience a little time spent mastering even the simplest knitting or dressmaking can quickly pay dividends. There are also companies which provide clothing kits consisting of material cut to size for the customer to sew together.

When buying clothes bear in mind how they are to be cleaned. The high cost of dry cleaning can be avoided by buying washable clothes.

Look out for sales. This may mean postponing your purchase or buying in advance, but a large portion of the price may well be saved. Think about buying second-hand, especially when needing children's clothes. Jumble sales, charity shops such as Oxfam and Save the Children are very good sources for bargains as well as other conventional second-hand markets. See also Family savers, page 77.

DIY

It is often difficult and expensive to obtain reliable workmen to do little jobs around the home. Labour rates are high and most tradesmen are more interested in the large contracts rather than a householder's small, low profit work.

More and more people are discovering that doing the job themselves can be the easiest solution. There is pleasure to be taken in a job well done as well as a lot of extra money in your pocket.

The DIY trade has advanced by leaps and bounds. Books of advice and all manner of products are now available for the home handyman to make the jobs easier.

The tricks for success start with planning and knowledge of what you are about to undertake. Far too many handymen come to grief when they say, 'I'll rip that off and see what's underneath.' Once 'ripped off' it may be too late to put it together again.

Find out what to do before you touch anything; there are many thorough books on the subject. Look through the DIY stores; there are always new products coming on to the market and you may find just what you need to save hours of work.

Do not rush a job: plan, check out the products, work carefully and success will be yours.

TELEPHONE

Do you know how much a telephone call costs? British Telecom's latest booklet, *Your guide to telephone charges* (November 1986), quotes one minute at 4.4p at peak time (9.00 am-1.00 pm). A five-minute chat during that period will cost four times as much as it would at the weekend, or between 6.00 pm and 8.00 am.

Provided the calls are absolutely necessary—as they often are—then it is not too important to know the actual rates. What *is* important is to know when the cheapest call can be made.

Phoning during standard or cheap rate periods makes economic use of the phone. For local, national, Irish Republic and mobile calls, the periods are:

Cheap Rate   All day Saturday and Sunday
                 From 6.00 pm to 8.00 am during Monday to
                 Friday

Standard Rate Monday to Friday only:
                 From 8.00 am to 9.00 am and
                 From 1.00 pm to 6.00 pm

Peak Rate   Monday to Friday only:
                 From 9.00 am to 1.00 pm

The rates and the periods in which they apply are complicated when international calls are made. The cost of an international call depends upon the destination, the length of the call, the time of day and the charge band for the country you are calling. More information is given in your phone-book or the *International Telephone Guide*, obtainable via Freefone BT1.

Here is a sneaky tip on how to give a quick telephone message to one of those people who simply will not put the receiver down once they start talking. Phone them just before their favourite TV programme begins, or during the advertisements in the show. You will get your message over and will not be kept hanging on!

Correspondence

If you cannot make your call at a cheap time, it may be cheaper to write a letter and many people make economies here too by reusing old envelopes. Certainly writing letters overseas is much cheaper than a telephone call. You can write to any EEC country for the price of a first class inland stamp.

TRANSPORT

Transport costs fall within two categories:

(a) Car expenses
(b) Other transport costs.

Reduce car expenses

1. Check yourself when driving and develop an economic technique.

   Most people are aware that fast acceleration, high speeds and hard braking push up petrol consumption and tyre wear—but it is still done.

2. Do not buy higher grades of petrol than your car requires, since this will increase costs. Check the handbook for the correct grade. Alternatively, do not go lower than the recommended grade—it may damage the engine.

3. Make sure that your car does not carry more weight than it has to. A large tool box in the boot, for example, increases the overall weight of the car and increases petrol consumption as well.

   Similarly, a roof-rack increases wind resistance, makes the engine use more petrol and takes even more money out of your pocket.

4. Ensure that maintenance is completed according to the vehicle's requirements. An out of tune engine, worn spark plugs or incorrect valve clearances result in an inefficient engine.

5. Organise lift schemes. Talk to your neighbours, friends and colleagues and see if you can possibly form a group to share travel to work, to schools, to shops, to stations and so on.

6. If you have a low use or weekend car, sell it! A car can always be hired for the occasional journey.

There is a lot of status attached to the size and power of cars which wastes both on the purchase and the running costs. When buying one, trim the size and power down to fit your requirements. There are many folk for whom a smaller car would be much more suitable, with negligible loss in comfort and significant positive increases in convenience and economy.

Reducing other transport costs

Use public transport. In a crowded city with a lot of traffic many people find travelling by underground with a season ticket cheaper and more relaxing than using a car, even if there are two or more people in it. Buses are also convenient and there are various types of travel card usable on both underground and bus. If you live in a suburban or country area you may find there is a local bus company which operates a cheap return ticket to any local destination.

Pensioners should take full advantage of relevant transport passes. Check out the schemes available at local bus operator's and British Rail information offices.

British Rail have some very cheap offers including the Family Rail Card. Once the annual card is purchased for a small fee and provided that at least one child makes the journey, the British Rail network of tracks is open to you at:

Two adults—half fare each on day returns
Each child—£1 per trip.

Take the strain out of travelling and save!

Ride a bike or walk.

Plan visits so that they can be made in one trip. For example:

   —photographs to be collected Monday
   —shopping required Tuesday
   —see the travel agent Wednesday
   —present to buy Thursday
   —hairdresser's appointment Friday

This looks as though five trips are needed. A little bit of patience, a phone call or two and a small delay, might result in all five jobs being done Friday with a single journey. A pocket notebook will help to keep track of jobs and to plan.

HEALTH AND LEISURE

If you look after your health and take sufficient leisure you will improve your overall well-being. Here are some recommended ways of doing this which are also aimed at saving you money.

Commerce, business and advertising present leisure and health in packages. Health farms, overseas holidays, expensive sports, leisure clothing, and health aids have their legions of company directors, marketing men, salesmen, advertising agencies, magazines and promotions, all after your money.

But the best things in life are free—as true nowadays as it ever was. If you want solid gold, real-time action of the most durable and impressive kind, look no further than out of doors.

Nature cannot be put into packets and sold through the shops. The best the world has to offer is freely available.

Outdoor pursuits are more popular than ever and represent a vast range of activities from drawing flowers to rock-climbing. There are many things for the individual or family to do. True that some activities are promoted by advertisements and some activities can be very expensive—but you takes your choice.

Something for all ages and temperaments is to be found in walking. It is an inexpensive recreation involving the purchase of waterproof outer clothes and some strong shoes or boots—all of which are as useful in towns in the winter as on top of Snowdon. The Countryside Commission estimates walking as the favourite outdoor activity for at least one-third of the population. This makes it twice as popular as all other organised sports put together!

Travel costs can often be shared or advantage taken of club outings. The Family Rail Card (see page 56) makes it very economical for the family to take long journeys by rail and senior citizens with their Rail Cards can travel anywhere by train at half price.

If your leisure activities include visiting theatres and cinemas, you should look out for cheap previews, half-price matinees. There are all kinds of price concessions for senior citizens and often for children too.

If drink and cigarettes figure largely on your budget, you can save a lot of money and improve your health, by cutting them down or even out!

Remember the public facilities provided by local councils. They have been provided for the public—use them and the facilities will grow even better. Most towns have a leisure centre, library, meeting hall and a museum. All these entertainments are inexpensive or free and well worth a visit.

And if bad health does come your way, ask if your medicines are cheaper to buy over the counter before you pay the NHS prescription fee.

Chapter 6
Budget

INTRODUCTION

Would you like to say, 'We can afford to go abroad this summer because we keep to our plan.' In other words, to know and be in control of your future?

A budget will help you to do that.

The budget itself is no more than a financial plan—a guide to your future income, expenditure and cash in hand. Much misleading information is given about budgeting but this is not the Cashwise approach.

The Cashwise budget is a simple cost plan—easy to prepare, tailored to personal requirements and accurate. It is a management tool designed to take the worry out of your financial future; to tell you how easy or difficult it will be to make ends meet.

If we were to prepare our budget from scratch—as some textbooks on personal and household finance tell us—we would have a lot of work to do. That is not our way. We shall use the Cashwise statement as the basis of the budget: the past as the key to the future.

When you possess the Cashwise statement showing one full year of income and expenditure you are in a position to make fairly reliable forecasts for the coming year. Basically, the cash flow patterns for the previous year will hold true for the next one, provided there are no major changes in your or your family's life. Inflation and wage increases must be allowed for; so too the significant 'one-off' purchases or receipts which are expected. In overall terms, a budget would look something like this:

	£
Last year's total expenses	10,700
Less: the 'one-off' cost of recarpeting the house last year	(2,500)

	£
Last year's regular expenses	8,200
Add: inflation at 6 per cent	492
deposit on new car	1,500
Budget of next year's expenses	10,192

And in very broad terms that is all that is necessary. To be of use, however, a budget must be far more detailed. With the Cashwise statement, detail and accuracy are at our fingertips.

BUDGET PREPARATION

The Cashwise budget is to be based on the Cashwise statement. These sheets contain your actual expenditure already categorised according to your particular circumstances.

If you have been following Cashwise closely, your finances should be in a well ordered, healthy condition. Careful completion of the Cashwise budget form for both income and expenditure will enable any cash surplus or deficit to be predicted in the forthcoming year. You can plan, therefore, when cash will be available for that new TV, car or carpet. Or, conversely, a predicted cash shortage will necessitate either cutting back on expenditure or arranging loan finance or another income.

To assist the preparation of your budget, the steps required have been incorporated in a budget working sheet. A blank of this document for you to copy is provided on pages 62-3.

Complete the income block first; last year's total figures goes into Column 1. Any 'one-off' income received in the last year is entered in Column 2. This is income not expected in the forthcoming year such as a legacy, capital sales, winnings or windfalls.

Subtract Column 2 from Column 1 and put the result in Column 3 which now shows the total annual income received regularly and forms the basis for the forecast of next year's income.

Column 4 is for any changes to income which are expected the next year. Cost of living increases, other rises, promotion and the like should be estimated and entered in this column, as should any foreseeable reductions in income. Note that any changes expected after the middle of the year should not be entered in Column 4. Since such changes affect only half or less of the forthcoming year, they are to be placed in Column 7.

The basic regular income (Column 3) plus or minus anticipated changes (Column 4) together give the forecast basic income to be entered in Column 5. Divide the Column 5 figure by 12 to obtain the monthly expected earnings to go into Column 6.

Column 7 is the place to put any significant one-off income. Make a note of the date the income is expected as well. Those increases expected on basic income but not due until after the half-year point are recorded here. Note the date from which the increases are expected to run.

A few steps that no doubt appear a little confusing when read, but which are easy to follow and understand when the task is actually being performed. Similar steps are followed to obtain the expenditure budget.

The total, last year's expenditure for each category chosen, is entered in Column 1. Column 2 is again the place for the exceptional items. This time one-off purchases are entered—these are significant expenses not expected in the forthcoming year. They would include the purchase of capital items: a car, major repairs or extensions to your home, costs of weddings, births, deaths and so on.

Column 1 (total expenditure) less Column 2 (one-off expenses) gives the regular, full year expenses to be entered in Column 3.

The forecast inflationary increase is entered in Column 4. The percentage of the forecast will, of course, change from year to year. The best place to look for the estimated inflation figure is in the specialist magazines such as *The Economist* or *New Society*. You will never be far out if the current inflation rate is used for your forecast.

It is impossible to be completely accurate when anticipating likely price increases. Some items will go up a lot, others may show small price rises—some may actually fall in price while others stay exactly the same. One can only ever hope for a very rough estimate.

Do not, of course, apply an inflationary increase to those items which never change. Some types of mortgage or loan repayments and HP payments, for example, will stay the same.

The forecast regular expenditure (Column 3) plus the effects of inflation (Column 4) tell us what our expected basic expenditure is going to be. Enter this in Column 5.

Divide the Column 5 figure by 12 to obtain the month by month expenses forecast and enter this figure in Column 6.

Column 7 is for the exceptional items. Such items are frequently difficult to estimate—or even foresee! Nonetheless, an attempt should be made. The checklist of household expenditure items on pages 24-6 will assist your memory.

Cashwise Budget—Working Document

Year:

For completion—see text.

Column	1 Previous Actual	2 One off	3 Regular (1−2)	4 Forecast	5 Forecast (3 + 4)	6 Monthly (5 ÷ 12)	7 One off
Income							
Expenditure							

Expenditure (cont.)

Cashwise Budget—Working Document

Year: 1987

Column	1 Previous Actual	2 One off	3 Regular (1−2)	4 Forecast	5 Forecast (3+4)	6 Monthly (5÷12)	7 One off
Income							
My salary	9360	−	9360	−	9360	780	+ 20 April
Joan's salary	1400	−	1400	+100	1500	125	−
Dividends	492	−	492	−	−	−	£93/quark
Sale of car	−	−	−	−	−	−	£1,800 Feb.
			11,252	100	10860	905	
Expenditure							
Groceries etc	1185	−	1185	+75	1260	105	
Butcher	220	−	220	+20	240	20	28 April
Milk/eggs	260	−	260	+28	288	24	
School meals	255	−	255	+33	288	24	see notes
Drinks	141	28	113	+7	120	10	see notes
Entertaining	425	65	360	−	360	30	see notes
Clothes	682	111	571	−	−	−	see notes
Newsagents	180	−	180	−	180	15	
My allowance	840	−	840	+120	960	80	−
Joan's allowance	390	150	240	−	240	20	
Bus fares	142	−	142	+38	180	15	see notes
Electricity	596	−	596	−	−	−	see notes

Expenditure (cont.)							see notes
Gas	410	—	410	—	—	—	see notes
Mortgage	2544	—	2544	—	2544	212	
Life assurance	336	—	336	—	336	28	
Rates – general	650	—	650	+50	700	—	see notes
– water	150	—	150	—	—	—	see notes
Telephone	202	35	167	—	—	—	£45/quarter
Consumables	107	—	107	+13	120	10	
Petrol and oil	253	—	253	+47	300	25	
Sundries – carpet	—	—	—	—	—	—	£500 March
– car insur.	130	—	130	—	—	—	£130 March
– garage	396	269	127	—	—	—	£75/quarter
– house insur.	175	—	175	—	—	—	£180 April
– dishwasher	276	276	—	—	—	—	—
	934		10011	343	8116	676	

Notes to budget calculation: 1987

School meals — adjusted for school holidays
Drinks — allow for Christmas and New Year
Entertaining — Christmas and New Year and that party in April
Clothes — adjust for the seasons and sale time
Bus, train and tube fares — calculate if a season ticket is worth having. Allow for holidays.
Electricity — quarterly payments with largest bill due February
Gas — quarterly from March
General rates — £65/month for ten months to March 1987, then £70 per month from May
Water rates — £80 due March and September

Regular payments expected to show small increases in the current year.
Have used the forecast increases, Column 4, to give a round month-by-month figure for the statement.

That new carpet will have to wait if the car is not sold in February.

The large part of the garage bill for 1986, the £269, has been taken out of the 1987 budget. Hope that the car can make it through the year!

Given small increase in house insurance for 1987 to cover for inflation.

When entering Column 7 items, do not forget to indicate the date the expense is likely to occur.

You have now completed the Cashwise budget working sheet. The Column 6 figures plus the Column 7 figures may be transferred to the Cashwise statement for the first six months of the year.

Where there is an exceptional Column 7 item for a particular month, simply add this to the regular figure budgeted for the month and enter the sum on the Cashwise statement.

For each month in the budget period, add down to find the closing cash balance; the estimated cash balance at the very beginning of the budget period being required to start the chain of balances going.

The cash balance at the end of each month is the best estimate of financial health over the coming year. If there is a surplus of cash at month end, you are winning. A deficit spells trouble and indicates that perhaps a revised budget—with less expenditure—may be required.

In business, such budget revisions may go on, it seems at the time endlessly. The universal problem is overspending. If this is your problem too, trim the budget. The budget then becomes your yard-stick or measuring device—make it work, stick to it and all will be well.

BUDGET IN ACTION

As the months pass and you are well and truly into the period, the actual income and expenditure figures are entered alongside the budget on the Cashwise statement. All well and good, but what use is it?

The budget represents your plan of action. If your actual expenditure and income roughly follows what is predicted by your budget, you do not have a problem.

But when the actual slips away from the budget, the financial alarm bells ring! So when your actual figures are known, compare them with the budget figures. Forget them if both figures are similar—when a large difference shows, however, you must find out why.

Broadly speaking, the budget and actual figures differ because either the budget itself is inaccurate, or the actual figures are affected by unforeseen expenses or income. A third possibility is a combination of both.

Whatever the reason, you need to sort out the difference and make a note back at Cashwise HQ of what has happened.

When the budget itself is incorrect, it is necessary to ensure that the same mistake is not made again in the following budget. Keep a record of what went wrong with sufficient details so that sense can be made of your notes in, perhaps, nine or ten months' time.

If the budget error is glaringly significant, do not be afraid of changing the relevant budget figures in the remaining months. But again, make a note of what you have done and why.

A large variance between budget and actual which is due to unexpected income or — more likely — unforeseen expense, is outside our control. A possibility of the event being repeated in a future budget period means that a note must be recorded at HQ. In this way, the budget statement will be tuned closer and closer to your particular cash lives — the budget becomes progressively more reliable and useful.

Variances between the budget and actual figures will result in either having more money than expected or less. Looking on the bright side, the variance may be an influx of money from winnings, a part of uncle's will, discovering a priceless antique in your attic or an extra income — we can but dream! No problem occurs here. Have a celebratory dinner and put the surplus money into a savings account until you decide what to do with it.

A variance which leaves you with less money than anticipated can bring the problems. Worry, hardships and the possibility of a crisis loom. This is dealt with below.

HELP!

The actual expenditure is greater than expected in your budget; you are made redundant; the car needs major repair; the water tank bursts in your attic. The cash is not available — what do you do?

Obviously there are degrees of cash crisis. For a small deficit, a budget revision may be all that is required. Look at the remaining budget and see where savings may be made. This will usually mean being strict with yourself for a while. The obvious targets are the luxury items such as drinks, smoking and entertainment. A little bit trimmed from the budget weekly soon adds up. Saving £10 a week for six months generates an extra £260 to tide you over.

Or if you prefer to take your medicine in one, strong dose, are there some items which can be cancelled or postponed altogether? A holiday, new car, new washing machine, the replacement carpet and the like may be possibilities for finding the extra cash.

Cashwise Statement

Year: 1987   Half Year: 1st/2nd

Month actual/budget	Jan a	Jan b	Feb a	Feb b	Mar a	Mar b	Apr a	Apr b	May a	May b	Jun a	Jun b	Total a	Total b
Income														
My salary		780		780		780		800		800		800		4740
Joan's Salary		125		125		125		125		125		125		750
Dividends		—		93		—		60		95		—		246
Sale of car		—		1800		—		—		—		—		1800
Sub-total (1)		905		2798		905		985		1018		925		7536
Expenditure														
Groceries etc		105		105		105		105		105		105		630
Butcher		20		20		20		20		20		28		128
Milk/eggs		24		24		24		24		24		24		144
School meals		18		24		24		12		24		24		126
Drinks		20		10		10		10		10		10		70
Entertaining		40		30		30		60		30		30		220
Clothes		30		50		100		100		20		20		300
Newsagents		15		15		15		15		15		15		90
My allowance		80		80		80		80		80		80		480
Joan's allowance		20		20		20		20		20		20		120

Expenditure (cont.)							
Bus fares	5	5	5	10	5	5	85
Electricity	-	250	150	-	150	-	400
Gas	-	-	150	-	-	100	250
Mortgage	212	212	242	212	212	212	1272
Life assurance	28	28	28	28	28	28	168
Rates – general	65	65	-	-	70	70	270
– water	-	-	80	-	-	-	80
Telephone	10	10	45	-	-	54	90
Consumables	10	10	10	10	10	10	60
Petrol and oil	25	25	25	50	25	25	175
Sundries – carpet	-	-	500	-	-	-	500
– car insur.	-	-	130	-	-	-	130
– garage	-	-	75	-	-	75	150
– house insur.	1	-	-	180	-	-	180
Sub-total (2)	727	963	1678	934	858	936	6118
Cash in Hand							
Opening Balance	100	278	2115	1320	1369	1529	100
Movement (1-2)	178	1835	(795)	49	160	(11)	1418
Closing Balance	278	2113	1320	1369	1529	1518	1518

Statement completed for half year budget only.

Cashwise Statement

Year: 1987 Half Year: 1st/2nd

Month actual/budget	Jan a	Jan b	Feb a	Feb b	Mar a	Mar b	Apr a	Apr b	May a	May b	Jun a	Jun b	Total a	Total b
Income														
My salary	718	780	756	780		780		800		800		800		4740
Joan salary	126	125	126	125		125		125		125		125		750
Dividends	—	—	93	93		—		60		93		—		246
Car sale	—	—	—	1800										1800
Interest	—	—	26	—										
Free-lance	59	—	1	1										
Sub-total (1)	963	905	1001	2798		905		985		1018		925		7536
Expenditure														
Groceries etc.	108	105	130	105		105		105		105		105		630
Butcher	19	20	15	20		20		20		20		28		128
Milk/eggs	24	24	21	24		24		24		24		24		144
School meals	20	18	24	24		24		12		24		24		126
Drinks	18	20	11	10		10		10		10		10		70
Entertaining	37	40	22	30		30		60		20		20		220
Clothes	29	30	—	30		100		100		20		20		300
Newsagents	14	15	16	15		15		15		15		15		90
My allowance	80	80	80	80		80		80		80		80		480
Joan's allowance	25	20	25	20		20		20		20		20		120

Expenditure (cont.)

Item									Total
Bus fares	12	15	17	15	15	10	15	15	85
Electricity	–	–	242	250	–	–	150	–	400
Gas	–	–	–	–	150	–	–	100	250
Mortgage	212	212	212	212	212	212	212	212	1272
Life assurance	28	28	28	28	28	28	82	82	891
Rates – general	65	65	59	65	–	–	70	70	012
– water	–	–	–	–	80	–	–	–	80
Telephone	11	10	14	–	45	10	10	45	90
Consumables	26	25	39	10	10	50	25	10	60
Petrol and oil	–	–	470	25	25	–	–	25	175
Sundries – carpet	19	–	–	–	500	–	–	–	500
– TV repair	–	–	–	–	–	–	–	–	–
– car insur.	–	–	98	–	130	–	–	–	130
– garage	–	–	–	–	75	–	–	75	150
– house insur.	–	–	–	–	–	180	–	–	180
Sub-total (2)	747	727	1529	963	1698	936	858	936	6118
Cash in Hand									
Opening Balance	(67)	100	149	216	2113	1320	1369	1529	100
Movement (1-2)	216	178	(528)	1835	(793)	49	160	(1)	1448
Closing Balance	149	278	(379)	2113	1320	1369	1529	1518	1518

Statement completed for half year budget and actual to February.

Perhaps the most satisfying way of overcoming such a shortfall is to draw from your savings. To do this, you will have to have savings to start with. Begin now! Plan to set a small sum of money aside each month until you have an emergency supply of cash. Just how much you choose to save depends upon the scale of your finances. This is very Cashwise—to put some money aside at normal times to tide you over difficult periods.

That is all very well but for many people, 'normal times' do not exist. The demands of a growing family, effects of inflation, running an essential car, furnishing your home, will not permit rainy-day savings to grow. In fact, the persuasive advertisements and easy loan facilities result in the normal state being one of debt. A varied collection of loans, credit sales, HP and a mortgage may have dispensed with some incomes for many years into the future. And what happens then?

Cutbacks are required: a holiday foregone or a large house to be sold, and the bailiffs, unfortunately, are finding plenty to do. More and more families are trapped by easy money.

In a crisis that affects the whole family, consult everyone. Discuss the best way to reduce expenditure or to increase income. Cashwise has a lot to offer and will bring financial order back to the family.

When all the possibilities of making reductions in expenditure have been examined, consider ways of increasing your income. A little extra may come in several ways:

— someone in the family finding part-time, or temporary work in addition to their usual activities;
— selling off some possessions but try to avoid selling personal items. Look through the classified columns of your local newspapers for ideas.
— taking in a lodger if you have a spare room.

One final option to bring you out of a cash crisis is to borrow the money. It is not easy to do this, however, when you have financial problems. The lenders will want to be satisfied that the repayments can be made.

Nonetheless, under certain circumstances borrowing may be the right thing to do. An immediate, large bill could be settled with a loan—the repayments coming from a revised budget or an extra, part-time income.

Be very careful; the act of borrowing to escape from crisis is frequently a way to even greater problems. Strict cash management is required.

The ways and means of borrowing are discussed in Chapter 9, *Financially Yours*.

RELAX

Whatever the magnitude and extent of your money problems, solutions are to be found by careful consideration of all the possibilities, thoughtful decisions, strict control over expenditure and detailed planning. If you are being pressed for money, a plan to show how you will make the repayments will engender confidence in the creditors — a compromise may be reached.

Anxiety, inaction and loss of temper achieves nothing at all. Let Cashwise help.

All in all, the best solution to money problems is not to let them arise. Follow the advice in Cashwise: budget wisely, do not overcommit yourself with loan finance and live within your means. Happiness may be just as — if not more easily — available to the poorer person than to the rich!

Chapter 7

Young Families

INTRODUCTION

Marriage changes the way lives are run; the arrival of children will make for more adjustments.

With one or more persons to consider, the individual appears to lose freedom. 'Not being able to do what they used to' is also aggravated by many other demands on the wallet or purse.

Money can become a major area for argument. Not making ends meet is a difficulty which will not pass quickly. A nagging worry can inhibit personal response and affection.

Certainly, personal readjustment is required—expectations have to be affordable. But Cashwise offers a practical way of coming to terms with controlling and planning the family's finances. With more skill and thought given to your finances, you may find room for a few luxuries as well.

THE THREEFOLD PATH

1. Extra income

This depends on job prospects, promotion, part-time work and so on, but even then this may well be a temporary solution.

Earning more may result in more money being spent at a faster rate; it is far easier to spend money than to earn it. Obviously some sort of plan and control is required to keep on top of all the demands.

Cashwise can provide the means of ordering your finances so that they look after themselves. The information is made available for discussion, rather than impassioned argument.

Check that all the DHSS family benefits to which you are entitled are being claimed. The following is a list of interest to the young family:

Child Benefit for children under 16 years or in full-time education

Family Income Supplement for parents with low earnings from full-time work

Supplementary Benefit for people over 16 years of age who do not have enough to live on

Child's Special Allowance for a woman whose marriage has been dissolved or annulled

Guardian's Allowance for parents who are looking after an orphaned child

Attendance Allowance for people who are severely disabled

Free Milk and Vitamins for expectant or nursing mothers and children below school age

Free Dental Treatment, Spectacles and Prescriptions for low income families

Free School Meals, Fares to School, School Uniforms, Clothing Grants, Educational Maintenance Allowances, Student Grants — ask at the local education office

Hospital Fares for people on low income.

Remember that eligibility for these benefits often depends on several conditions being met. To find out more about any of these items, check for the relevant leaflet at your local library, post office or branch of the DHSS. If you think that you are eligible, enquire at the DHSS office.

2. Spend less

Easier said than done! A new family and possibly a new house can create a bewildering time. Not only are there more frequent demands for your time, you may be besieged by bills from all quarters: food, clothing, rent or mortgage, medicines, petrol, garage charges, decorating costs, gas, electricity, milk, TV licence, house maintenance, a vast range of 'essential' consumer goods and the like.

You would like to save but cannot see how to do so. Cashwise can help by showing just where the money ends up. A little understanding goes a long way.

Knowing where it has gone is the first step in overcoming money shortages. With the relevant figures right there your grasp of the problem will be strengthened and ideas will come. Cashwise provides many money saving ideas.

Initially, the Cashwise statement can be used to pin down all the details of your cash flow. An easy way to start is to write down what you spend every single day, for a week or two. With a little practice, you will find that a selection of critical figures from key areas will provide the necessary control. The Cashwise budget enables a plan to be made so that your requirements can be satisfied without frustration or strain.

Put money arguments behind you—know what you are doing and talk out any problems with the facts at your fingertips.

3. Be realistic

The trick is not so much to turn dreams into reality, but to have the kind of dreams that are more easily realised.

Frustration has two sides, namely:

(a) the desire which motivates and
(b) the ability to achieve that desire.

So be realistic about your expectations.

FAMILY SAVERS

With so much money being spent in all directions, the young family needs to find ways to save. Parents naturally wish to do the best they can for their offspring. Where food, warmth, education and medicines are concerned the money is well spent. Anything which satisfies a child's 'real' needs is to be encouraged.

However, a lot of effort and money is often expended on appearances—on presenting children in the best possible clothing. This is not of itself very productive. The child is usually indifferent to this effort. It is done by and for the parents. New and expensive items are bought for the baby, the cot, swinging cradle, pram, pushchair, clothes and toys. Many of these goods have a useful life of only months. They may then be sold for a fraction of the original cost. Baby remains indifferent to the effort—he or she wants mum and dad, feeding and a regular, clean nappy.

If mum has to go to work to pay for all these new expensive items and spend less time with the child, it seems a little illogical. For the loving parent who is short of cash, the second-hand market has many bargains. If you have not paid so much for the baby's kit and clothes, you do not mind when the baby ruins them!

Second-hand 'baby' shops are doing good business. Classified columns in local newspapers and the 'for sale' cards in newsagents and supermarkets will also show you the stock on offer. Take pleasure in obtaining quality buys for so little money and pass the pleasure on to the baby.

Children often outgrow clothes before wearing them out. Bear this in mind when clothes shopping for them.

For the older as well as younger child, toys are another target for second-hand buying, especially when you have experienced expensive Christmas toys being broken before the Christmas lunch is served. The markets are as before, but you will have to be very quick off the mark to make a purchase prior to Christmas—second-hand toys are snapped up. Do not be put off by a few failures, be persistent. Other times of the year are easier to buy in—and cheaper.

Forward planning pays when you buy from sales or a non-Christmas, less active toy market. (If you buy in advance make sure that the toys are well hidden.)

In our gadget-ridden age, entertaining children can become expensive. Help your children to develop interests which are inexpensive—and sociable. Swimming, bird-watching, Cubs, Brownies, Guides, Scouts, country walks, adventure pursuits, reading, camping and so on are all relatively gadget-free and cheap. Many clubs are crying out for new members.

FRANKNESS

When money is in short supply in a family, this is a problem to be shared and solved by the whole family. Do not let it become one person's burden.

Sitting on a problem and trying to keep a smile on your face so as not to upset anyone, is a recipe for disaster. 'The whole is greater than the sum of its parts' is just as true for the family as for anything else. Be frank, explain any problems, ask for help and let the family rally round.

Cashwise can help a lot here. Discussions will not progress far without facts. Cashwise's records properly maintained and presented will clear the air, open the door to fruitful discussion and show how to plan your way out of trouble.

If you are a housewife dependent upon a 'housekeeping allowance' from your husband, Cashwise can do the arguing for you when more money is needed. Inflation means that your money does not buy as much this year as it did last year—Cashwise will show this.

National figures for household expenditure are based on averages taken from thousands of families. They do not mean much when applied to any particular family—we are all unique. Cashwise provides the facts and figures for your family, your expenses, your lifestyle. These figures are all the arguments you need when asking for a housekeeping rise.

Chapter 8
The Self-employed

INTRODUCTION

The attractions of greater independence and freedom draw many would-be entrepreneurs to become self-employed. Statistics show that they represent about 10 per cent of the work-force. The general conception is that they enjoy above average earnings, but in fact about 70 per cent of small private businesses fail within the first few years.

Although the reasons for failure are manifold, money can never be far away from any difficulties. An understanding of the use and behaviour of cash is an essential requirement for success.

Cashwise can offer much assistance. By applying Cashwise to personal finances, skill and insight is gained in the handling of money. Learning how to make economies and how to make the most of cash may mean the difference between failure and success when the going gets rough.

Another way in which Cashwise will help is by direct application to the business. Although Cashwise is presented as a household and personal finance control system, the basic design is identical to that used in sophisticated management report packages. Both the Cashwise statement (see page 28) and the Cashwise budget (see page 59) are easily adapted to the small business.

Note that Cashwise is not a substitute for financial accounting; Cashwise is designed for internal control purposes—to help you to run a business better. There is, however, little extra work involved in preparing the Cashwise statements from run of the mill bookkeeping routines.

BUSINESS CASHWISE

The annual or half yearly sets of financial accounts are prepared for those with outside interest in your business—most notably the taxman.

A business, however, also requires regular, usually monthly, statements of performance for internal control and efficiency purposes.

Cashwise will provide an analysis of business costs and cash flow information invaluable for the effective management a small business needs in a competitive environment. The basic methods of Cashwise given in this book will apply equally well to Business Cashwise. What will change, however, are the categories of income and expenditure used in the statements.

The 'source documents' are again receipts and invoices and may be stored temporarily in a 'current month' envelope. After the receipts have been sorted and sub-totalled, store them as before in a manilla envelope for each month. Your accountant will need these documents so do not throw them away. Keep them in their envelopes, he will appreciate the orderliness of the paperwork. Keep all source documents — no cut-offs now!

The categories used in the expense analysis will not be the same as those used in the household Cashwise. Choose categories appropriate to your business. Petrol, van maintenance, tools, rents, telephone, materials, clothing, etc may, for example, be suitable for the odd-jobbing carpenter or plumber.

To select categories, list just where the money goes in the business. Choose the categories from your list.

Business income is frequently very simple — it comes from one source, the customer. Where you are selling something or providing a service, income may be shown on the Cashwise statement as 'Sales Receipts'.

The full Cashwise statement showing income, expense and cash balance for each month is really a crucial document. Knowing what the business cash flow looks like will help to keep you away from bankruptcy. After a few months of operation, the statements will give an idea of what the regular business income and expenditure should look like. Any divergence from the regular pattern should set alarm bells ringing in your head. What does the divergence represent? How did it arise? If it is dangerous, what can be done to stop it? If it is favourable, how can it be maintained?

This is what business management is all about!

And when it comes to planning, the Cashwise budget is at your disposal. By the time one year has passed, the Cashwise statement will be finely and accurately tuned to your business. What better base could be found when you want to plan?

With the budget entered on to the Cashwise statement in the second year of operation, you have a strict but flexible method of ensuring that your plans succeed. All the budgetary control tips provided for household financial control will work just as well for the small business.

Any changes in methods, cost reductions, advertising or marketing which affect cash flow will be revealed—and assessed—by the Cashwise statement. This is an effective, reliable indicator of business performance.

Another way in which Cashwise can help the small business is by highlighting the cumulative effect of the small but regular costs. Postage stamps, telephone calls, stationery, low cost materials, short trips to town, small tools, unimportant repairs and other 'insignificant' items, soon add up and have a disproportionate effect on profit. Any cost, however small or unimportant, is a straight deduction from profit.

PROJECT ASSESSMENT

The layout of the Cashwise statement and budget forms makes them ideal for a budget cash flow to assess propositions. By completing the forms with your estimated figures, the projected cash life of a project is quickly revealed.

Turnstone Engineering, for example, is offered a contract for 90,000 toggle pins to be delivered 15,000 a month for six months. The contract price is £280 per thousand pins. The usual price for 1000 pins has been £180 and so Turnstone Engineering were overjoyed with the contract.

Now this is a two-man business operated out of a garage. Resources are very limited and the production capacity has never been more than 12,000 toggle pins a month. Nonetheless, for such a lucrative contract, both partners feel prepared to work around the clock if necessary and really get the business moving.

To make 1000 pins, they reckon on paying £60 for materials, £40 for the labour and about £10 for the electricity used in the machines. This information came from their regular Cashwise statement which they had adapted for their own use. Also, each month, the partners draw £700 for their own expenses and other overheads.

So they estimated their profit on the contract to be as follows:

	£
Contract price	
90,000 pins at £280/1000	25,200
Less: Manufacturing Costs:	
Labour	
90,000 pins at £40/1000	3,600
Material	
90,000 pins at £60/1000	5,400
Electricity	
90,000 pins at £10/1000	900
Total Manufacturing Cost	9,900
Overheads	
6 months at £700/month	4,200
Total Cost	14,100
Profit Estimate	£11,100

This pleased the partners so much that they finished early and went for a drink. They said that would give them the money they needed for expansion. The only cash in hand the business possessed was £6200 in a building society.

In their enthusiasm, however, they had failed to take note of all the terms of the contract, the small print. Had they read the contract carefully they would have seen that payment was promised in full at the end of the six-month delivery period.

So what? The £11,100 profit estimate would still be theirs, and that's a fact.

But what happens to their cash flow is a different matter altogether. In truth, the partners are heading for the bankruptcy court as the statement shows.

Not that they should abandon the contract altogether: it will make a profit after all. What they need to do is either to renegotiate the terms of payment or apply for a loan to carry them over the difficult period. As small businessmen they could apply for a government secured loan through their bank manager. Up to £75,000 could be available with 70 per cent of the sum borrowed secured by the Loan Guarantee Scheme.

WORK AND PLEASURE

With a business operated from home, care must be taken not to mix business and household finances. It is difficult enough to obtain a clear view of a business performance without the complications of running a house mixed in.

Keep the two sets of receipts separate and operate two distinctly separate Cashwise systems. Where a facility has both a business and a domestic use, make sure that the proper receipts are kept among the business records. Business statements and, notably, tax deductible costs come under close scrutiny and require proper justification. A note on a slip of paper will do to operate the household Cashwise.

When business income is not regular, say in the case of a contractor who may have to wait many months for payment, acute cash shortages may arise. The bills, however, will not wait and you could be faced with a string of business and household bills to settle, but no money coming in for a few months.

A neat way to smooth over the troubled waters of irregular income, is to open a budget account at a bank. See *Bill spreader*, page 13.

DO NOT FORGET

When the basic Cashwise statement has been mastered, a next step for the self-employed would be to turn the statement into a proper account. To do this properly, all income and expenditure must be included and the cash-in-hand balance will reconcile to the cash box plus bank balance.

In other words,

	Total Month's Income
Less:	Total Month's Expenditure
	Cash Surplus or (deficit)

To make such an account work, some skill is required. The difficulties arise when the cash surplus or (deficit) at month end is reconciled to the physical cash plus that in the bank. There are many reasons why the statement balances will not agree with the actual money available.

Transactions such as cheques, direct debits, standing orders and the like, may be included in one set of figures but not the other.

Charges may be deducted from the bank statement but not from the

Cashwise Project Analysis

Project Description: 90,000 toggle pins
— 6 month contract

Date: 24/4/8X

Month	1	2	3	4	5	6
Income						
Payment in full ~ month 6						25,200
Sub-total (1)	1	1	1	1	1	25,200
Expenditure						
Material	900	900	900	900	900	900
Labour	600	600	600	600	600	600
Electricity	150	150	150	150	150	150
Overheads	700	700	700	700	700	700

Expenditure (cont.)						
Sub-total (2)	2,350	2,350	2,350	2,350	2,350	2,350
Cash in Hand						
Opening Balance	6200	3850	1500	(850)	(3,200)	(5,500)
Movement (1-2)	(2,350)	(2,350)	(2,350)	(2,350)	(2,350)	22850
Closing Balance	3,850	1,500	(850)	(3,200)	(5,550)	17,300

Note how bankruptcy in month 3 follows from this profitable deal!

Cashwise Project Analysis

Project Description:

Date:

Month																
Income																
Sub-total (1)																
Expenditure																

Expenditure (cont.)																						
Sub-total (2)																						
Cash in Hand																						
Opening Balance																						
Movement (1-2)																						
Closing Balance																						

Cashwise statement. This would be due to interest deductions, bank charges and commission.

And there is always the possibility of a mistake—simple to make but very difficult to locate and correct.

Hence, to use Cashwise as a full account needs painstaking effort and attention. Unless you have a few numeric skills, the full accounts preparation may be best left in the hands of an accountant. Cashwise presents the information you require quickly and 99 per cent accurately—this is enough for any business decision. You could engage an accountant to worry about the 100 per cent accuracy and, even then, the orderliness and presentation of the paperwork will save time, which should be represented in lower fees.

And finally, a few broader considerations that will affect the cash lives of self-employed persons. There is less security than for salaried employees. What happens to your business, for example, if you are unable to work due to ill-health or injuries? There are insurance policies available to see you over such periods which are well worth considering—it is reassuring to know that if you are physically unable to work, there will still be an income.

Another way to look after yourself is to make sure that any medical problems are dealt with quickly and efficiently. And because of the long waiting lists for some NHS treatment, this implies private medical care. You could pay for private treatment yourself but even rich men must shudder at the thought of paying out for major surgery. For the average self-employed person, a private medical scheme such as BUPA is more suitable. There are also the cheaper, half-way schemes such as the PPP (Private Patients Plan) which will provide private treatment if NHS treatment is not immediately available, or an overnight allowance if it is.

With a longer view of the self-employed person's prospects, a private pension is a good investment. Ensure your standard of living when you are older and take the pressure off retirement by joining one of the private pension schemes now. Contributions to such schemes are tax deductible for self-employed persons—see Chapter 9, *Financially Yours*.

Advertisements for self-employed insurance schemes, health plans and pension schemes are to be found regularly in the daily and weekly press.

Chapter 9
Financially Yours

INTRODUCTION

Cashwise itself is designed to be a management tool to assist the day-to-day running of your personal and household finances. The outside world of banks, building societies, insurance companies, finance houses, pension schemes, investment brokers and the tax man, affect our cash lives as well. This chapter outlines the services and requirements of these institutions and explains just how they affect our cash lives.

For the purposes of this discussion, the various financial institutions are considered to assist the average individual in one of three stages in his or her life, namely:

Struggling — when the money will not go far enough and the wolves are at the door.

Planning — perhaps the most common stage; comfortable, but with one eye on the future.

Investing — a rare and bountiful period when all of life's money requirements have been satisfied but the loot keeps rolling in.

STRUGGLING

Even after all the good money sense, economies and forward planning of Cashwise have been enacted, and the piggy bank raided, is there still not enough money? The expensive, unforeseen bill or sudden loss of livelihood can bring a cash crisis to the most well planned and smoothly run household.

The first recommendation is to apply Cashwise to your finances. Use the Cashwise statement to find out the real picture of your money lives, make the economies suggested, use the budget to plan your recovery and devise your own ways of economising or making a little extra.

The second suggestion is to borrow—provided that you have good control over the plan for repayments and that the money borrowed is for a specific purpose. If your finances are in a mess and you do not know what you are doing, it will be difficult to find anyone willing to lend money.

Loans are not made out of someone's goodness of heart to help people in distress. They are made as a business and the profits come only when the repayments are made. If you look like a bad risk, you will not be lent a dime.

When the cause of the cash crisis is a large sum of money which has to be paid out in the near future, borrowing is acceptable. A plan for the repayments needs to be made even if the plan exists only in your head; better still use the Cashwise budget to schedule the repayments and find out if something else has to be done to make ends meet.

It is in your own interest not to borrow unless you have a reliable plan to make the repayments. This point must be stressed because of the large number of families and individuals who are put under great strain by deceptively easy credit.

Borrowing became more widespread during periods of high inflation which have occurred over the past 15 years. 'Live now and pay later' made more sense during inflationary periods by:

— enabling purchases to be made at current lower prices;
— turning rapidly wasting money into goods; and
— making the real value or purchasing power of the repayments fall.

High levels of inflation do not apply at the time of writing. If the repayments seem a heavy burden this year, they may still be the same heavy burden in three years' time.

Another reason for borrowing is that saving is so difficult. The legal authority of a loan contract ensures that repayments will be made in those households where money tends to be spent as soon as earned.

Even when a nest egg has been accumulated, there may be reluctance to let it go since it may never be saved again. Whatever the reasons, loans and credit buying are more popular than ever.

Choosing a small to medium-size loan

Once you have decided to borrow and are satisfied that the repayments can be made, what are the criteria for the many types of loan? These depend upon:

— the size of the sum borrowed;
— what the loan is to be used for;
— the security offered;
— the length of repayment period required.

The most important point to bear in mind when shopping for a loan is its real cost. Do not pay too much attention to the advertisements offering incredibly easy and cheap money. You are dealing with businessmen who plan to make a profit at least somewhere along the line.

The full cost of a loan is given in a single figure, the Annual Percentage Rate of Charge, or APR for short. This is the figure you want to know before taking out a loan. If this figure is not obvious in the loan documentation, ask for it.

The APR enables a quick and meaningful comparison to be made between the different types of loan available. Although the interest rates and, hence, APR, vary naturally month by month, company by company, the sources of borrowed money may usually be ranked as follows, the cheapest coming first:

— Mortgage; top-up mortgage or second mortgage (for large sums);
— Bank personal loans;
— Finance company personal loans;
— HP and credit sales;
— Trading cheques and vouchers.

Bear in mind that rates of interest applied to a loan may be either fixed or variable. With a fixed rate of interest, the size of the repayments will not change—the same repayment sum will be paid back over the entire repayment period.

If the rate of interest on a loan is quoted as being variable, you are gambling a little since the repayments might become smaller, or they may increase.

Details of loans, APRs, repayment periods, sums to be lent and so on may be found in advertisements in the daily press or in pamphlets direct from the relevant institutions.

Having thought about whether a loan is really necessary, your ability to meet the repayments and the types of loan on offer, we enter the money market with a wary hand on our signature pen.

If you have had a bank account for some time without gaining any black marks, your bank manager may grant you an overdraft. This permits you to be overdrawn on your account up to a certain limit.

Overdraft facilities are particularly useful when money is a problem for a short period. The salary or wages paid into the account at month end may significantly reduce or even remove the overdraft — and the interest to be charged. And towards the middle or end of the month, the account still has the overdraft facility for you to fall back on. Interest will be charged on any overdrawn balances.

In the short term, overdrafts are cheap and flexible. Tax relief is not available on the overdraft interest paid unless the overdraft is for business use. A disadvantage of the overdraft is that it may be cancelled at short notice and any overdrawn sums demanded back by the bank manager who is responding to tougher lending conditions or who is suspicious about your credit worthiness. Overdrafts can be formalised into loans.

Another, more permanent, solution for a smallish sum is the short-term loan. Repayment periods may be anything up to five years.

Within this category, borrowing from a friend or relative could be included: not to be recommended but it does happen. Even with this type of loan, a formal written agreement is worth having to make sure that no misunderstandings arise. Good intentions are not reliable when money is at stake. Money problems have a habit of getting a lot worse before they improve, and a few friendly faces are very reassuring; so don't lose them!

The bank personal loan may be available provided you have sufficient security and can prove your ability to make the repayments. Suitable security would include property, stocks and shares, and insurance policies.

The bank personal loan is generally easy to arrange and is cheap. You do not necessarily require an account at the bank to be eligible for such a loan. The rate of interest is fixed so that the total cost of the loan is easy to calculate. Repayments are usually made in equal monthly instalments by a standing order from a current account.

Another choice is the bank ordinary loan account. Repayments may be spread over a period up to five or seven years, dependent upon the amount borrowed and the purpose of the loan. The interest rate is variable like that of an overdraft. The bank ordinary loan account will be more expensive than an overdraft, which is reduced monthly when salaries are paid in.

The all too easy loan facility available by not paying the full amount due on a credit card statement is very expensive. Cards such as Access and Barclaycard can give the best part of two months' free credit between purchase and payment date—a debt allowed to run on is to be avoided because of their high rates of interest. No interest is payable on purchases listed on a statement provided settlement is made in full and your payment reaches them within 25 days of the date of the statement. Any amount outstanding at the end of the 25 day period will attract interest from the statement date and interest will continue to be charged on a daily basis until full repayment is credited to your account.

Various types of credit are used to encourage you to buy at the large stores. These may appeal if you shop regularly at one store anyway, but they will limit your freedom to shop around. Stores accounts are described in Chapter 1.

Other types of credit available are numerous and generally more expensive than a bank personal loan. Such schemes would include moneylenders, credit brokers, finance company personal loans, trading cheques and vouchers. Check each APR on offer and compare it with a bank personal loan.

Mail order shopping is a popular alternative to crowded shopping centres and busy stores. For those who are infirm, armchair shopping is a necessity. The credit facilities on offer through catalogues are similar to the ordinary shop accounts. Mail order goods, however, tend to be expensive but one way to offset this is to become an agent yourself. As an agent you earn commission on all the sales made including your own, but not all mail order companies offer agencies.

Last but by no means least are the perennial hire purchase and credit sale. There are three guises:

HP	True hire purchase in which the ownership of the goods does not transfer to the customer until all the payments have been made.
Conditional sale	Similar to HP in that the goods title is transferred only after full payment. Here, however, there is no element of hiring.
Credit sale	The easy payment scheme in which the property rights to the goods pass to the buyer at the very start.

Being very easy to obtain at the time of choosing goods, these types of credit are very popular. They are expensive though, and even 'free' credit has costs which can be avoided by the cash customer able to shop around.

Choosing a large loan

Large sums of money may be borrowed on long-term loans with repayment periods from five to 25 years. Building societies and banks are the main sources of long-term loans.

Security is usually a property or a property improvement. The availability of such money is governed to a certain extent by the finance markets in general and the level of savings in particular. There are also the company's regulations to be complied with before an advance is approved.

A large, secured loan is the cheapest way to borrow money for buying a house or for major home improvements. It is not a recommended source of small loans because of the cost of setting up the mortgage.

These are, of course, mortgages, which is the name given to a loan which has property as its security. A second or top-up mortgage may be taken on a property whose first mortgage represents only a fraction of the house's full market value.

Mortgages are available from building societies, banks and through the services of a mortgage broker. Tax relief is not available on the majority of loans, but money borrowed to buy or improve your home or that of a close relative is eligible.

Business loans; buying your own home; making permanent improvements to your home; buying or improving the home of a former wife or husband; buying or improving the home of a dependant relative and, for people over 65 years old, buying an annuity secured on their own home: these are the qualifying loans for which tax relief is available on the interest paid. But there is no relief on loans over £30,000 for buying or improving homes.

The government have removed restrictions on the use of mortgaged funds. House owners with unused equity may now borrow up to 70 per cent of the value for any purpose—at a rate 3 or 4 per cent above the standard mortgage rate.

When borrowed money is required for several purchases, make sure that any potential qualifying loans are put to good use. For example, a Mr Jones wished to build a fourth bedroom on to his home and to buy a new car all in the same year. He had enough money to pay for either the bedroom or the car but not for both. He planned to have a loan.

Mr Jones should apply for a top-up mortgage to build his bedroom because, not only will the interest rates be lower on the mortgage, but the mortgage will qualify for tax relief on interest paid. He can then pay for the car in cash.

STILL NOT CLEAR!

All the doors are closed to you and still there is not enough money. At the best this may simply mean a postponed purchase; at the worst a lot of trouble.

When you are being pressed to pay off a debt and there is definitely no money available from any source whatsoever, you must plan. Creditors will listen to genuine cases of hardship and may accept an authentic, realistic repayment plan. They do not have a lot of choice!

Show your income and a regular sum that you can afford to give them to clear the debt within a reasonable period—and keep your fingers crossed.

If you are taken to court, you may be able to get legal assistance and the leaflet 'Legal Aid could help you' is what you need to see. This leaflet should be available at your local library or Citizens Advice Bureau.

PLANNING

This is probably the situation in which the majority of folk find themselves: neither in the grips of a cash crisis nor rolling about in surplus money. With a little freedom of choice, they wish to know the best things to do.

A cavalier attitude to live for today is all right for the young, but there is good sense in making small sacrifices now so that the future is more prosperous and secure.

Forethought can usually ease the troubles of those bad stretches which can crop up in anyone's life. This is the approach to planning adopted in this chapter—not to become millionaires but to ensure that money problems do not plague our future lives; that the future will be better, or at least not as bad as it could be.

Planning will include house purchase, pensions, coping with redundancy, taxation, savings, insurance, wills, trusts and deeds of covenant to give a bright future to those you care about when you've finished.

House purchase

In Britain home ownership is a popular goal to free yourself of rent and leases and as a sound investment. All in all, money spent on buying a house will satisfy many dreams although this may not be apparent during the first years.

The first house will be just about all that can be afforded. The mortgage repayments make a very large hole in income and then rates, furniture, heating, decorating, maintenance, electric gadgets, telephone and the garden take the rest. The initial years are difficult and many people who lived through them wonder now just how they managed. They did manage, and quite frequently enjoyed the time as well.

In a period of high inflation, a large mortgage repayment may diminish but as inflation is reduced, a large monthly mortgage repayment can remain a heavy burden for a much longer period. In the long term, a house of your own is usually a sound investment.

When choosing a house, let your personal preferences be the first guide. You need to consider the size of the mortgage you could afford, number of bedrooms, distances to places of work and schools, the neighbourhood and locality and the general condition of the property. Take time to look at many properties with several estate agents and do not compromise yourself at all. The right house will come along if you wait—a rash purchase of a house can be regretted for many years.

It is also important to consider the future prospects of the house and the area in general. A motorway built at the bottom of your garden would adversely affect your health and house value. The stages of buying a house ensure that a search is conducted to find out if the house value is likely to be affected by local building or civil engineering work. The house is, after all, security for the mortgage and the mortgagee is only protecting his interest. But you yourself have a part to play by keeping your eyes and ears open. The employment prospects of local firms is an important factor at the current time. Large-scale redundancies in an area will make the house market stagnate. Whispers of distant plans to build airports, new estates, roads, factories and so on, will all have a bearing on your purchasing decision.

Obtaining a mortgage is a straightforward process provided you have a steady income or, if self-employed, can show reliable profits over the previous three years. The money available to be lent out by building societies and banks is an important factor and varies considerably from time to time.

Lending rules do vary a little but roughly speaking, the mortgage made available to you will depend on:

- some multiple of income. For example, you may be able to borrow 2½ or 3 times a sole applicant's income or 1¾ to 2 times the total income of joint buyers.
- the purchase price or valuation of the house, whichever is the lower. Eighty or 90 per cent of this figure is usually lent but up to 100 per cent may be available to first-time buyers or on a brand new property.

So it is worth shopping around.

There are two popular types of mortgage; repayment and endowment. Both are available over 10 to 25 year periods or up to retirement age.

The repayment mortgage is a straightforward loan paid back in instalments of both principal and interest.

With an endowment mortgage, the interest and an endowment policy premium make up the regular repayments. At the end of the mortgage's life, the endowment matures and pays off the mortgage principal. This type of policy is available with or without profits on the endowment policy.

Provided that the mortgage is a 'qualifying loan' (see *Taxation* on page 103), the interest repayments are eligible for tax relief under both mortgage schemes.

To improve prospects of obtaining a mortgage, place some savings with the bank or building society you choose to use. Enquire whether they operate special schemes for prospective mortgagors. One scheme, for example, guarantees a mortgage after you have saved with the institution for at least one year. The mortgage allowed is a multiple, say 10 times, of the balance in the savings account. So if you manage to save £2000 in one year, you could then apply for a mortgage of up to £20,000.

The process of obtaining a mortgage is expensive in itself. After selecting a house and obtaining approval for a mortgage you will have to pay:

1. *Legal costs.* The actual fee charged will vary according to the complexity of the purchase, the scale used and property value.

This pays for transfer of the property title, conveyancing.
- Search and enquiry to ensure that a trouble-free title to the property will be yours;
- Land registration which depends on the property value and any prior registration;
- Sources of finance have legal aspects to be enacted;
- Stamp duty which is levied according to the purchase price of properties over £30,000.

Always ask your solicitor for an estimate of these costs.

2. *Estate agent's charges.* If you are selling a house through an estate agent, the fees are charged at around 1½ or 2 per cent of the selling price of the property. Check before commissioning an agent to act for you.

3. *Surveyor's fees.* A surveyor values the property, provides a thorough report on the property's condition and completes a comprehensive survey, which you should see. The actual fee charged depends on the amount of work done and the property's value.

4. *Removal expenses.* A cost not to be underestimated, which is dependent upon the quantity of possessions to be transferred and the distance involved.

   The removal expenses may be reduced by hiring a suitable vehicle and enlisting the services of two or three able bodies. Not a way of saving recommended to those who own large properties!

5. *Property insurance.* A wise precaution, and compulsory if the property is mortgaged.

Insurance

Insurance has the appearance, unfortunately, of consuming money without benefit. Some hold by this view. There are also countless others who have had to face minor trouble or catastrophes and were very happy that at least part of their problems had been covered by an insurance policy. Misunderstandings about the actual insurance cover purchased and reported delays in settling claims may have turned some minds against insurance.

Terms and available cover vary from company to company so shopping around is important. An insurance broker has a part to play here and can quickly show you those policies most suited to your circumstances.

The sort of insurance policies of interest to the average family would include:

- Home contents
- Buildings
- All risks
- Motor
- Life
- Personal accident
- Legal costs and expenses
- Holiday
- Freezer
- Sundry specialised policies usually related to sport and leisure pursuits such as small craft, caravan, riding.

It is particularly important for parents to take out some kind of life assurance to cover the death of one or both of them, in order to safeguard their families.

Bear in mind the effects of inflation on life assurance and any insurance policy.

Life cover, building insurance, building contents insurance, and general possessions insurance all need to be revised regularly to maintain their purchasing power. Some policies are index-linked; that is they automatically increase the cover and the premiums to keep in line with inflation. Others may give the option to increase cover if you so wish.

Bring insurance into your plans; few policy holders regret their decision. Further details are available from the offices of insurance companies themselves or from insurance brokers. Remember, however, that insurance companies have a vested interest in their policies and insurance brokers are paid commission, so neither group is likely to offer impartial advice.

Taxation

Taxation has extensive impact and will be an integral part of our planning. Whatever our income, the Inland Revenue may want a share.

Before taking their percentages, however, they do permit some tax-free income in a system of allowances and deductible expenses. Claims for allowances and the permitted expenses or 'outgoings' are made on the annual tax return alongside statements of your earnings.

The actual value of an allowance varies and is fixed by the Chancellor of the Exchequer. All that you have to remember to do is to make the appropriate claim. Allowances are discussed in greater depth below.

The outgoings are deducted from your gross income before tax is calculated. Any expenses incurred necessarily as part of a trade, business or profession may be deducted—although these are the subject of many disagreements with the Inland Revenue. The most common outgoings include interest paid on mortgages or business loans, subscriptions to trade or professional organisations and the use of a vehicle in a business.

So for each tax year which runs from 6 April one year to 5 April in the next, the basic tax assessment is as follows:

	Gross Income
Less:	(Outgoings)
	Net Income
Less:	(Allowances)
	Taxable Income

It is the 'taxable income' which is used to calculate tax due. At the time of writing, the Revenue take 27 per cent of the taxable income as the basic rate tax. Higher tax rates apply in bands to larger and larger amounts of income.

You are notified of your tax liabilities in a Notice of Assessment. In most cases, tax due relates to current year earnings. The most common exception is investment income in which tax is not deducted at source. This is assessed for tax on a previous year basis.

The Pay As You Earn (PAYE) system collects tax from each salary or wage packet. It is the job of a tax collector to make sure that the tax paid under PAYE agrees with the total tax due as shown on the Notice of Assessment. Any under or over payments of tax are adjusted at year end.

Completing the tax return can be a major task. It is not wise to conceal income from the Inland Revenue since they will cross check their records from many sources. Any doubts about eligibility for allowances or the suitability of outgoings are best kept to yourself—claim them and let the Inland Revenue decide. There follows a summary of income, outgoings and allowances which will assist you to complete a tax return:

Gross income

Salaries and Wages. Tax usually deducted at source under PAYE.

Interest received. Tax may have been deducted at source (as with a building society) so check the terms of the investment.

Stocks and shares. Tax usually deducted at source and the amount of tax paid is shown on a 'tax credit'.

Rent receivable. To be declared for tax but 'outgoings' will usually reduce the tax burden.

Social Security benefits. Most of these remain tax free with the notable exception of unemployment benefits.

Pensions. Usually liable for tax.

Outgoings

These are expenses incurred which the Inland Revenue permits to be deducted from gross income before tax percentages are applied.

For most people, outgoings are of two types

1. Those related to a job, profession or business; and
2. those which are related to 'qualifying loans'.

Type 1 outgoings are eligible expenses that are 'necessary' and have been incurred 'wholly' and 'exclusively' for a trade, profession or business.

Examples of these outgoings include:

- tools specific for a trade;
- a car's expenses, and if the car has mixed business and pleasure use, then a proportion of the expenses are used;
- protective clothing for a trade or profession;
- fees and subscriptions paid to societies or organisations relevant to the trade, profession or business;
- reference books;
- expenses for part of a home provided that part has an exclusive business use;
- travelling expenses incurred while following a trade, profession or business. (Note that travelling costs to and from work are not permitted.)

The commonest outgoings are of the second type, interest payable on 'qualifying loans'. Such loans include mortgages to buy or permanently improve your own home, the home of a former and now separated husband or wife, and the home of a dependent relative. Loans taken out to maintain or repair such a property without 'improving' that property, will not qualify (see page 96).

Other outgoings include alimony, maintenance payments and covenanted payments. Also, for persons over 65 years of age, a loan used to buy an annuity secured on their own home will qualify.

Allowances

Allowances are not directly related to incurred expenses as outgoings are; they are deductions from net income which are allowed because of an individual's personal circumstances. The amounts of the allowances are fixed in the Finance Acts and are made automatically upon correct completion of the tax return when the requirements are met. The most common allowances are for the single person, the personal allowance, and for a married man, the married allowance, and earned income allowance for a wife. Most married working couples will pay less tax when they combine their income for tax purposes. This is because the allowances for two separate incomes are

> Single Man's Personal Allowance
> and
> Woman's Personal Allowance;

whereas if they marry and combine their allowance, they receive

> Married Man's Allowance
> and
> Wife's Earned Income Allowance.

And the married man's allowance is much bigger than an individual's allowance.

If both marriage partners are high earners, their combined incomes may pay higher rates of tax on the top end of their salaries. In this case, they can opt for separate tax assessments to avoid paying this higher rate tax. Other allowances include:

- Housekeeper's Allowance for the widow or widower who has a live-in relative or employee helping about the house;
- Dependent Relative Allowance which may be claimed if you support an old or infirm person or a mother or mother-in-law;
- Son or Daughter Services Allowance may be claimed if you are over 64 years of age and are depending on the services of a son or daughter;
- Additional Personal Allowance for the single parent;

- Age Allowance which replaces the personal allowances for those over 64 years old;
- Additional Age Allowance for those over 80 years old;
- Widow's Bereavement Allowance which is claimable in the year of death of the husband and in the year after;
- Blind Person's Allowance.

Allowances are also given for payments made into superannuation and pension schemes, and life assurance policies taken out prior to April 1984.

Redundancy

Few would actually plan to be made redundant, but redundancy is a threat hanging over many people's plans. Some employers give more than the statutory minimum redundancy payment and those who receive it have no legal grounds for complaint.

Those who have or have been promised only the minimum payment may be interested in the following information. The minimum redundancy payment formula depends on:

- the employee's age;
- his or her 'continuous service' with the firm up to a maximum of 20 years; and
- the amount of the normal weekly pay.

The figures used in the calculations may change from time to time and it is wise to make sure that the latest information is at your fingertips. Ask for the revised leaflet 'The Redundancy Payment Scheme' from your local office of the Department of Employment.

Tax is not applied to redundancy payments below a certain figure— £10,000 at the time of writing.

Not every worker is entitled to redundancy payments. The exceptions are those who:

- have not worked for the employer for more than two years;
- have actually been dismissed for other reasons such as inefficiency or poor health;
- are self-employed;
- are under 18 years of age; or
- are over retirement age.

There are other exceptions, the details of which will be found in 'The Redundancy Payments Scheme'.

Pensions

Planning one year ahead may be enough for some folk, although others plan 10, 20 or 40 years ahead when they join pension schemes. The state pensions are too low to maintain most people's standards of life uninterrupted after retirement—many plan to have extra income from a private pension scheme.

By making sufficient National Insurance contributions, anyone over retirement age can collect the basic state pension. The retirement ages are 65 years for a man and 60 years for a woman—although these are likely to change. The state pension has two parts,

- Basic pension,
- Additional retirement pension.

The basic pension is available to anyone with sufficient contributions whereas the additional retirement pension is given to those who:

- were not self-employed and
- whose employer operated a pension scheme which had not opted out of the state scheme.

The state pension is index linked so that it will always have roughly the same purchasing power. For most workers, the basic pension is theirs automatically provided they have sufficient contributions. There is a growing number of workers who spend a few years working overseas and unless they contribute at least to Class 3 of the NI options, their pension rights may be affected.

In addition to the state pension scheme, many employers offer private pension schemes to their staff. Their terms vary from company to company and you are advised to ask your personnel office for details of the scheme operated at your place of work.

Such schemes are called 'Occupational Pension Schemes' and may be either contributory or non-contributory. Take each scheme at face value but there is no point in joining if:

- The benefits are poor;
- You change jobs frequently so that contributions do not accumulate with one firm; or
- You are planning an early retirement.

Some schemes permit additional voluntary contributions to be made and since all such contributions are eligible for tax relief, they represent a sound way to save. Remember, however, that your additional savings may not be available before retirement.

And there are more schemes to come! A growing market of personal pension schemes is available to anyone but will be of particular interest to the self-employed, those without occupational pensions and those with some regular freelance earnings. For it is only to these classes of people that tax relief is available on contributions to personal pension schemes.

With all pension scheme contributions, the amount of tax relief given depends on an employee's 'net relevant earnings'. So if you already contribute to another scheme, you may have used up all your 'net relevant earnings', having none to spare for other schemes and hence no more tax relief on contributions.

Provided that they are eligible for tax relief, all contributions to pension schemes have the beauty of reducing the amounts paid to the Inland Revenue. A £100 contribution, for example, is all for the pension scheme and your future, whereas if you do not contribute:

£73 stays with you, and
£27 goes in income tax at current rates.

So it would be wise to plan to retirement age and join some private pension scheme, if you have not already done so. When calculating the amounts of money you wish to have in retirement, remember:

- Inflation may reduce the purchasing power of a pension both before and after you retire so plan for a surplus or use an index-linked pension scheme;
- Some of your present expenses will have gone altogether, for example, mortgage repayments, loan repayments, cost of travelling to and from work, clothes for work and so on;
- Money may be made available to you from other sources such as expiring insurance policies and legacies.

For retired home owners, the Home Income Plan is attractive. Basically, a loan is taken out with the home used as security. This loan is then used to buy a life annuity from an insurance company which provides the extra income. Upon death, the loan is repaid out of the estate before capital gains tax is levied. This is suitable for people of 70 or over who have no plans to move house.

Wills and trusts

At a time of bereavement, the relatives may be subject to much unnecessary strain if there is no will. Any family, especially a business family or partnership, can face unimagined difficulties when sharing out the estate of a person who died intestate.

Dying and leaving a will means that your estate goes where you wish and the act of distribution is quicker and less expensive. Appointing an executor speeds the process along.

To leave a legacy to a minor you will have to create a trust and nominate a trustee or trustees. The same procedure is used to provide someone with an income but no capital rights.

The job of drawing a will, creating a trust, naming an executor or a trustee, is best undertaken with professional advice. Solicitors and high street banks offer these services. The Consumers' Association has a good book to guide someone through these difficult periods, *What to do when someone dies*. It includes information on funeral costs.

Deed of covenant

A deed of covenant, by the way, may save tax if you make payments to your children. Provided that your children are either over 18 years old or married, a covenanted benefit made to them for a period of at least six years is tax deductible. For each covenanted benefit paid an eligible offspring may claim back from the Inland Revenue basic rate tax calculated on the payment. If your child already pays tax, no tax refund will be due but covenanted payments are not liable to higher rates of tax. Deeds of covenant are recommended if you are or will be supporting older children at college or university. Relevant forms are available from the Inland Revenue. Remember that student grants are reduced if a student's total income exceeds a set level — check this with your local authority since the rules are complicated.

INVESTING

With Cashwise to guide you, the advance of years may reduce the strain of mortgage, the cost of house furnishings, cars, overseas holidays, medical contributions and so on. Life is often not quite that generous but, even so, a time may arise when you have surplus money. What do you do with it? There are many luxuries you could indulge in or you could take out an investment portfolio.

But before you embark on an investment career, make sure that you and your family, if you have one, enjoy financial security. A home of your own, life assurance cover and an adequate pension take priority over other investments. Remember that tax relief may be available on pension scheme contributions and mortgage interest payments.

You may wish to invest for capital growth if you are not short of day-to-day cash. Alternatively, an extra monthly income could be yours. Countless variations of investments exist.

First of all, even humble savings accounts come in many guises: saving accounts, deposit accounts, higher interest rate account, lump sum accounts, fixed term accounts, treasurer deposits and a host of others. Naturally, you wish to obtain the highest interest rates available but these accounts offer a range of other facilities. In practice, the choice of account is easy, being determined by such factors as:

- How do you wish to save, by monthly or irregular lump sum payments?
- Do you wish to have easy access to your money or could you leave it untouched for months?
- How much money do you have?

And by deciding each of these questions, you will find that your choice is narrowed to one, two or three accounts. Details of actual savings accounts are available from branches of building societies and banks.

The interest rates quoted for such accounts may be given under a variety of names such as:

Net rate	—which is the actual percentage of interest paid into an account.
Gross rate	—means that interest is paid without tax being deducted;
Equivalent rate	—tells you what the interest rate is really worth to the basic taxpayer;
Compound annual rate	—is the equivalent rate which is compounded annually thereby allowing for quarterly and half-yearly interest payments.

For a little more adventure with your investments, trust funds may be the answer. Your money is pooled in a fund together with that of all other investors to the trust and is then invested across a wide range of shares by professional managers.

There are many trust funds and they are listed, together with their prices and yields, in the *Financial Times*. Broadly speaking, you may wish for a growth trust, to give capital growth; an income trust, for an extra income; or an income/growth trust, to give a balance between the two.

There is a choice as to the type of investments the fund makes: property funds, UK investments, European, American, Japanese, new industries, general trusts, select trusts and many more. The full range of trust on offer may be found by following the investment advice offered by daily newspapers, specialist magazines or the high street banks.

Even professional trust managers can be wrong. Your money placed in their hands is in a risk business—prices may rise or fall. The choice is yours.

Chapter 10
Tail-Ends

INTRODUCTION

This chapter describes ways in which the basic Cashwise can be put
to more sophisticated, though still very practical, use.

Advice and methods are given on how to turn Cashwise into an
authentic account which will be of interest to those who wish for even
greater control. A simple method of reconciling bank statements is
also covered.

CASHWISE GRAPH

The Cashwise graph is simple to prepare, easy to read and provides
solid gold insight into your financial health. When you have operated
Cashwise for a year and have prepared a budget, then a graph presents the whole story at a glance!

Without slipping into abstruse formulae or time-consuming detail,
three graph lines will be all we need. And each line will plot on the
same axes or scale.

Make the scale on the vertical axis show the cumulative expenditure for one year. The example on page 112 makes this clear; see how
the scale runs from zero at the bottom up to just over the estimated
total annual expenditure at the top. Label this axis 'cumulative
expenditure'.

The horizontal axis has 12 divisions, one for each month in your
Cashwise year. Starting with the first month in your Cashwise year
on the left, enter each month in succession. Label the axis with the
year it represents:

'1987'
or 'April 1987 to March 1988'
and so on.

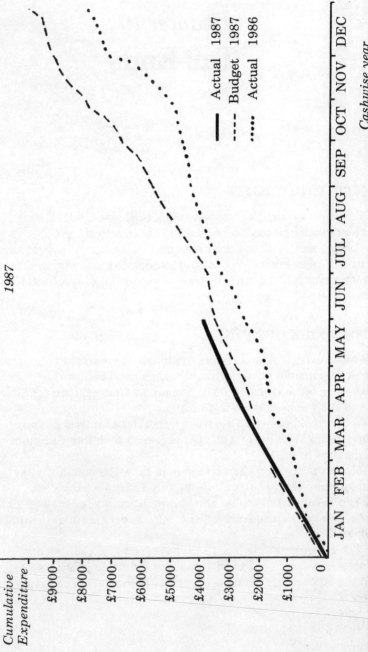

Cashwise graph: Actual, Budget, Previous year

1987

Cumulative
Expenditure

£9000 —
£8000 —
£7000 —
£6000 —
£5000 —
£4000 —
£3000 —
£2000 —
£1000 —
0 —

JAN FEB MAR APR MAY JUN JUL AUG SEP OCT NOV DEC

Cashwise year

——— Actual 1987
– – – Budget 1987
······ Actual 1986

If in doubt, study the example provided which has a total budget expenditure of £10,000 and a year which corresponds to the calendar year. And on the graph are three lines:

1. Budget cumulative;
2. Actual expenditure—last year cumulative; and
3. Actual expenditure—current year cumulative.

When the graph is prepared, the budget and last year's actual expenditure figures are available on your Cashwise statements. The figures will be given month by month and not cumulatively. To find the cumulative figures, simply add on each month to the previous month's cumulative. For example, the budget for each of the first four months in 1987 is as follows:

1987 Budget

January	—	£500
February	—	£650
March	—	£920
April	—	£600

To turn these into cumulative figures within 1987, January's £500 stays the same but by February the cumulative expenditure will be:

January's £500 + February's £650 = £1,150

March's cumulative budget expenditure will be:

February's cumulative £1,150 + March's £920 = £2,070.

And so on, so that the first four months' cumulative budget expenditure for 1987 are:

1987 Budget cumulative

January	—	£500
February	—	£1,150
March	—	£2,070
April	—	£2,670

Plot the cumulative figures against the respective month on the Cashwise graph.

Do the same for last year's actual expenditure but make sure that the graph line you draw is readily distinguishable from the cumulative budget line. Different colours or a different type of line are required—see the example.

Year: 1987

Cashwise Statement

Half Year: 1st/2nd

Month actual/budget	Jan a	b	Feb a	b	Mar a	b	Apr a	b	May a	b	Jun a	b	Total a	b
Income														
My salary													4816	4740
Joan's salary													767	750
Dividends													240	246
Sale of car													1620	1800
Interest													61	—
Free-lance													127	—
Sub-total (1)													7631	7536
Expenditure														
Groceries etc													710	630
Butcher													93	128
Milk/eggs													136	144
School meals													141	126
Drinks													95	70
Entertaining													311	210
Clothes													315	300
Newsagents													78	90
My allowance													480	480
Joan's allowance													120	120

Expenditure (cont.)											
Bus fares										94	85
Electricity										341	400
Gas										290	250
Mortgage										1270	1272
Life assurance										168	168
Rates – general										282	270
– water										74	80
Telephone										102	90
Consumables										77	60
Petrol and oil										214	175
Sundries – carpet										470	500
– car insur.										130	130
– garage										211	150
– house insur.										176	180
– TV repairs										19	–
Sub-total (2)										6397	6118
Cash in Hand											
Opening Balance										(67)	100
Movement (1-2)										1234	1418
Closing Balance										1167	1518

Statement completed to show half year results only – see 'change analysis'.

The graph now gives you a quick visual presentation of how your budget for the forthcoming year compares with actual expenditure last year. The other line to plot is the cumulative actual expenditure for the current year. This line may be plotted month by month as you calculate your actual expenditure—do not forget to cumulate the figures.

The example takes one nearly half-way through the year and the current actual expenditure has been cumulated and plotted to May 1987. See how the actual expenditure is creeping above the budget—care must be taken if the 1987 budget is to be met. Current expenditure took a sudden rise in March, far more than in 1986—why was that? It is necessary to check it out.

Use the graph to keep you up to date with the overall picture of your cash flow. And when it comes to asking for more housekeeping or a rise, or when reviewing the state of your finances, use the power of these graphs.

RELATIVE CHANGES

As they are given, the simple subtracted difference between two figures is readily visible on the Cashwise statements. So if one item has a budget of £25 and the actual expenditure is £29, you can see at a glance that £4 over budget has been spent.

This simple subtraction or 'absolute' difference does not always tell us enough. Consider the differences between these two sets of figures, all with an absolute difference of £10.

Set A	Set B	Difference
£50	£60	£10
£1	£11	£10
£1,980	£1,990	£10

Now if set A was the budget and set B actual expenditure, there would be no need for concern if £1990 had been spent instead of the budget for £1980—not much relative or percentage change here.

When £11 is spent instead of £1, there is, however, some need for concern!

Relative or percentage change between figures as well as the absolute change must be considered. Here are the percentage changes between Set A and Set B above:

Set A	Set B	Percentage that Set B bears to Set A (as $\frac{B}{A} \times 100$)
£50	£60	120
£1	£11	1,100
£1,980	£1,990	100.5

In the percentage or relative figures, the £1 to £11 difference amounts to a 1,100 per cent change which is significant. To highlight both the absolute and relative change, a Cashwise 'Change Analysis' has been provided. A blank for copying is provided on page 119.

The Change Analysis statement will provide useful comparisons between the following figures:

actual expenditure current year;
budget expenditure current year; and
actual expenditure last year.

INCOME/EXPENDITURE ACCOUNT

Cashwise is a tool for controlling personal and household expenditure and income. The information is accurate and tuned closely to your specific requirements.

For those who want to, however, the Cashwise method and format is easily converted into an authentic income and expenditure account. Extra control is gained and a little more information and this may be required for a tight budget or the home business.

Broadly speaking, the Cashwise statement is the same except that every last penny of income and expenditure is shown. For each monthly accounting period, the opening balance of cash in hand or at bank, plus the month's earnings show all the money available to you in that month. Deduct from this figure the month's expenses to obtain the closing balance of cash in hand or at bank.

In other words:

	Opening Balance for month
Plus:	Income earned during month
	Total Money at your disposal
Less:	Expenses for the month
	Closing Balance for the month

Cashwise Change Analysis   *Year: 1987*
                                              Half Year: 1st/2nd

Comparisons   A—actual against budget.
               B—actual against last year's actual.

Comparison	A —	A %	B —	B %
Income				
Total				
Expenditure				
Total				

— subtracted difference; ie budget — actual

% percentage difference; ie $\dfrac{\text{actual}}{\text{budget}}$ x 100

Cashwise Change Analysis

Year: 1987
Half Year: 1st/2~~nd~~

Comparisons A—actual against budget.
B—actual against last year's actual.

Comparison	A —	%	B —	%
Income				
My salary	76	102	142	118
Joan's salary	17	102	(8)	98
Dividends	(6)	98	11	112
Sale of car	(180)	90	—	—
Interest	61	—	17	—
Free-lance	127	—	—	—
Total	95	101	162	115
Expenditure				
Groceries etc.	(80)	113	3	99
Butcher	35	73	21	82
Milk/eggs	8	94	(5)	106
School meals	(15)	112	(10)	107
Drinks	(25)	136	22	128
Entertaining	(91)	141	(48)	122
Clothes	(15)	105	(26)	111
Newsagents	12	87	(5)	106
My allowance	—	100	—	100
Joan's allowance	—	100	—	100
Bus fares	(9)	111	11	92
Electricity	59	85	(63)	118
Gas	(40)	116	(15)	105
Mortgage	2	100	4	99
Life assurance	—	100	—	—
Rates — general	(12)	104	(17)	105
— water	6	93	(8)	108
Telephone	(12)	113	9	94
Consumables	(17)	128	(11)	121
Petrol and oil	(39)	122	(27)	116
Sundries - carpet	30	94	—	—
- car insurance	—	100	—	100
- garage	(61)	141	(18)	117
- house insur.	4	98	(5)	103
- TV repair	(19)	—	—	—
Total	(279)	105	(188)	104

— subtracted difference; ie budget — actual

% percentage difference; ie $\dfrac{\text{actual}}{\text{budget}} \times 100$

The closing balance for one month becomes the opening balance for the next month. Not one penny is to go astray!

A bank current account provides a useful check on the month end balances. Without too much difficulty, all income and expenditure may be passed through a bank current account, though only in total figures. At each month end, the Cashwise statement's income and expenditure account will agree with the current account's balance—well, except for unfinished transactions. Ensure that the bank statement is issued a couple of days after month end to catch all the month's cheques and other transactions.

It will be very unlikely for the two statements to agree exactly. Differences arise and must be used to bridge the gap between the two balances in a reconciliation. Differences will be due to:

— Cash in hand, drawn out of the bank but not spent and consequently not shown on the Cashwise statement;
— Unpresented cheques which have been drawn and shown as expenditure on the Cashwise statement but have not yet passed through the current account;
— Bank charges and interest paid on loans will be deducted from the current account but not from the Cashwise statement;
— Standing orders and direct debit mandates which may be charged to the current account but not the statement; and
— Cash income which may be included on the Cashwise statement but may not pass through the bank.

A reconciliation will account for differences such as these and perhaps others until both balances are proved to agree. Obviously much care is required when preparing the Cashwise income and expenditure account, for one small mistake may be extremely hard to find. All in all, for most purposes the greater accuracy and stricter control obtained from such an account is not worth the effort! Use the Cashwise statement to record 95 per cent of your cash flow and you will probably meet 99 per cent of your information requirements anyway.

CHEQUE BOOK RECONCILIATION

One reconciliation that most people have to make is that between the balance shown on cheque book stubs and a bank account statement. It is very useful to keep a running total of your bank balance on the cheque book stubs, but what is done when that balance disagrees significantly from the current account balance? Write off the difference and start afresh?

With a little practice, balancing both figures is achieved without much difficulty. The following steps will help you.

Cheque numbers

Look for the latest cheque number shown on the bank statement and write this down at the top of a rough piece of paper. Consult your cheque book to find the balance on this cheque's stub and write this figure on the paper alongside the cheque number. This figure and the bank statement balance are the two balances to be reconciled.

From this starting point, add or subtract down the rough piece of paper until the bank balance is obtained, looking out for:

Receipts

These are easier to deal with than withdrawals since there are usually fewer of them. Are there any receipts shown on the bank statement which you have failed to include on the stubs? If so, show them as a 'Plus' line on the rough paper.

Standing orders

Have all the standing orders shown on the bank statement been deducted from the stubs? If no, show them as a 'Less' line on the reconciliation.

Unpresented cheques

Look through the cheque numbers listed on the bank statement to make sure that all those you have written out have in fact been presented. An unpresented cheque will be a 'Plus' line.

Other charges

Are there any other deductions on your bank statement which are not reflected in the stubs? Such charges may include direct debits, bank charges, interest and commission. To bring these items into the reconciliation, show them as a 'Less' line.

Show each individual figure on a separate line and record enough information for you to understand the action you have taken in one or two months' time. Now, provided there are no arithmetical or transcription errors, the two balances should agree. If they do not agree, check your arithmetic on the reconciliation statement and in the cheque book stubs. Keep your eyes open for any missing items, bad figures, items entered twice, transcription errors and so on.

A typical reconciliation statement would look like this:

		£
		£
	cheque number 100072	267.39
Less:	standing order on insurance	(21.00)*
Plus:	unpresented cheque 100069	110.00
	100066	15.00
Plus:	investment income	92.00 *
Less:	bank charges	(3.50)*
	commission	(9.00)*
Agrees to bank statement		£450.89

Make a note of where your corrections are made as follows:
* above
(21.00) + 92.00 + (3.50) + (9.00) = £58.50
added to cheque number 100073.

This is so that you know what you have done when you refer back next month. The other items, unpresented cheques, should clear themselves.

A neat copy reconciliation statement above, plus the note of the corrections made, should now be written out on the front of the bank statement if there is room — if not, put it on the back. This reduces the amount of paperwork filling your drawers!

TAIL PIECE

Cashwise will bring your money under your control with the minimum amount of work. The common-sense, economic habits suggested in the various sections will save you much on your expenses.

The purpose of Cashwise is to improve your life by giving you that ease and assurance which come from knowing exactly what you are doing. Sort out your finances, put them in their place so that they look after themselves. Whether you are well off or hard up, there is more to life than money. Health and happiness can be largely independent of the stuff, so make yourself truly Cashwise — be efficient and prudent with your money resources and never let them become a problem.

Appendices

Appendix 1
Summary of Banking Services

The following is a summary of banking services most likely to be of use to the individual. New services are being added all the time and they are available from the high street banks such as Barclays, Lloyds, Midland, National Westminster, Royal Bank of Scotland, Co-operative Bank, Trustee Savings Bank and others.

The National Girobank offers similar services through the nation-wide network of post offices. And also, major building societies now offer a wide range of banking services.

CURRENT OR CHEQUE ACCOUNT

The most useful type of account which comes with a cheque book, instant withdrawal facilities, regular statements and access to many other facilities such as standing orders or direct debits. By arranging for a salary to be paid directly into such an account and by making full use of the cheque book, the cheque account will deal efficiently with 90 per cent of your cash transactions.

Interest is not usually earned on a credit balance in a current account. Certain banks do offer a cheque account with interest but such an account often has to have a certain minimum balance, such as £1000.

STANDING ORDER

The standing or banker's order is an instruction to the bank to make a payment of a fixed sum to a named recipient (usually to the bank account) on a given day. The orders may be made on a particular day of each month, say the 28th, to pay such monthly bills as mortgage, rates, life assurance premiums, loan repayments, HP payments and so on.

The order could also be made quarterly, half-yearly or annually to pay other less frequent bills.

This is a very useful facility which relieves you of having to memorise and enact the payments.

DIRECT DEBIT

This is similar in operation to the standing order except that the recipient instructs the bank concerning the amount of money to be withdrawn from your account. This appears to be a strange state of affairs but remember that you, as the account holder, have to sanction the direct debit mandate in the first place and that you would, of course, give it only to those organisations or individuals that you trust.

This is useful for those regular bills which vary a little in amount. Annual insurance premiums on index-linked policies, subscriptions to professional or trade organisations, certain mortgage repayments and so on are the type of bill to be settled by a direct debit. The billing authority notifies the client of the sums charged by separate notification.

CASHCARD

The plastic identification card which gives access to the 24-hour cash dispensers available at most major banks and some building society branches. Available to current account holders on application.

CREDIT CARDS

More of the 'plastic money' which can be used at a very large number of outlets, from buying petrol at your local service station to a romantic dinner in a Roman restaurant. Available to account and non-account holders on application.

Useful and harmless provided the outstanding amounts can be settled as and when they arise.

DEPOSIT AND SAVINGS ACCOUNTS

A range of accounts exist which give interest on credit balances. In general, higher rates of interest are available in return for one or more combinations of the following:

— A period of notification prior to withdrawal;
— Larger sums deposited;
— Regular monthly savings; and
— Fixed term deposits.

See *Investing* in Chapter 9, *Financially Yours*.

BUDGET ACCOUNT

A specialised account which permits large bills to be settled as and when they occur in exchange for fixed, monthly payments into the budget account. For a complete description of this type of account see *Bill spreader* in Chapter 1.

OVERDRAFT AND LOAN FACILITIES

The bank personal loan account or an overdraft on a cheque account represents some of the cheapest borrowed money available. Being available for a wide range of purposes and easy to set up, this type of loan is not as widely used as it ought to be. See *Choosing a small to medium-size loan*, page 93.

MORTGAGES

As building societies actively encroach into banking territory, so too are banks pursuing the mortgage customer. Regular mortgages and specialised mortgage saver schemes are offered. See Chapter 9.

SAFE DEPOSITS

Most banks offer this service for a small charge and it is a good idea for storing valuable documents, but you can also use your solicitor's services.

TRAVEL FACILITIES

There has been over recent years an enormous growth in both the volume and the range of services provided. Nowadays not only do the banks provide the traditional traveller's cheques and foreign currency but also eurocheques, credit cards, travel insurance, personal medical insurance, holiday finance and more.

For a complete guide to these services which are changing yearly, enquire at your local bank.

Appendix 2
Electricity Consumption Data

The following consumption data uses Electricity Council figures. Consumptions quoted are the averages for typical appliances and give the units of electricity used. The cost per unit to you will be found on your last electricity bill.

KITCHEN

Cooker	To cook one week's meals for the average family uses about 17 units.
Cooker hob	Bacon and egg breakfast for four uses about ½ unit.
Radiant boiling ring	Chicken stew for four takes less than ½ unit.
Conventional oven	24 scones cooked for 1 unit.
Fan oven	48 meringues cooked for 1 unit.
Cooker grill	1 lb sausages for less than ½ unit.
Cooker hood	10 hours' use for 1 unit.
Crêpe maker	139 crêpes for 1 unit or 12 sessions each making 8 crêpes.
Deep fryer	5 lb chips for 1 unit.
Contact grill	25 well done steaks for 1 unit.
Microwave oven	3 lb joint of beef cooked for less than ½ unit.
	4 chicken pieces for ½ unit.
Multi-purpose cooker	Lamb chop casserole for four people for ½ unit.
Rôtisserie	3 lb chicken cooked for under 1½ units.
Sandwich toaster	38 sandwiches for 1 unit or 6 sandwich making sessions for a family of four for 1 unit.

Slow cooker	8 hours' use for 1 unit. Beef casserole for four cooked for ½ unit.
Toaster	70 slices of toast for 1 unit.
Yoghurt maker	71 yoghurts for 1 unit.
Ice cream maker	15 hours' use for 1 unit.
Hot food trolley	More than 1 hour's use for 1 unit.
Hot tray	1½ hours' use for 1 unit.
Blender	500 pints of soup for 1 unit.
Can opener	Several thousand cans opened for 1 unit.
Carving knife	More than 200 joints carved for 1 unit.
Coffee mill	50 kg coffee ground for 1 unit.
Coffee percolator	75 cups of coffee for 1 unit.
Food mixer	More than 60 cake mixes for 1 unit.
Kettle	12 pints of boiling water for 1 unit.
Instant water heater	More than 3 gallons of hot water for 1 unit.
Knife sharpener	15,000 knives sharpened for 1 unit.
Waste disposer	50 lb rubbish disposed of for 1 unit.
Refrigerator	One day's use for about 1 unit.
Refrigerator with frozen food storage	One day's use for about 1½ units.
Freezer (upright)	1 to 2 units per day.
Fridge/Freezer	About 2 units per day.
Dishwasher (cold fill)	One full load—2 units.
Extractor fan	24 hours' use for 1 unit.
Fluorescent strip light (40W)	About 20 hours' use for 1 unit.
Floor polisher	4 hours' polishing for 1 unit.

LAUNDRY

Washing machine (automatic)	Weekly wash for a family of four takes about 5 units.
	9 lb cottons (with pre-wash) washed at 90°C for 2½ units.
	4 lb synthetics washed at 50°C for less than 1 unit.
(twin-tub)	Weekly wash for a family of four—12 units.
Tumble dryer	9 lb cottons and towels dried for less than 2½ units.
	4½ lb synthetics dried for less than 1½ units.

| *Spin dryer* | 5 weeks' use for 1 unit. |
| *Iron* | 2 hours' use for 1 unit. |

LIVING ROOM

Television (colour)	22 inch gives 6-9 hours' viewing for 1 unit.
Stereo system	8 to 10 hours' listening for 1 unit.
Tape recorder	More than 24 hours' playing for 1 unit.
Lamp (100W)	10 hours' illumination for 1 unit.
Lamp (60W)	16 hours' illumination for 1 unit.
Vacuum cleaner	Cylinder type gives 1½ hours' use for 1 unit. Upright type gives 2 hours' cleaning for 1 unit.
Convector heater (2kW)	½ hour's warmth for 1 unit.
Fan heater (2kW)	½ hour's warmth for 1 unit.
Oil-filled radiator (500W)	2 hours' warmth for 1 unit.
Panel heater (1.5kW)	40 minutes' warmth for 1 unit.
Radiant heater (3kW)	20 minutes' warmth for 1 unit.
Heating pad (30W)	More than 30 hours of operation for 1 unit.
Slimline storage heaters	A 2kW model will use 45-75 units per week during the heating season. Larger models use proportionately more.

BEDROOM

Single overblanket	All night long for seven days uses 2 units.
Single underblanket	Used for 1½ hours each night for one week, takes less than 1 unit.
Double overblanket	All night for a week uses 3 units.
Double underblanket	At 1½ hours per night for a week—less than 1½ units.
Health lamp (100W)	10 hours' operation for 1 unit.
Hair dryer (500W)	12 ten-minute sessions for 1 unit.
Hair rollers	More than 20 hair do's for 1 unit.
Hair curling tongs (30W)	60 half-hour curling sessions for 1 unit.
Tea maker	35 cups of tea for 1 unit.

BATHROOM

Shower (7kW)	A 3-5 minute shower taken seven days a week uses 3 to 4 units.
Shaver	1 unit gives 1800 shaves.
Towel rail (250W)	4 hours' operation for 1 unit.
Infra-red heater (1kW)	1 hour's warmth for 1 unit.

WORKSHOP/GARAGE

Battery charger (12v)	30 hours' charging for 1 unit.
Extension lamp (100W)	10 hours' illumination for 1 unit.
Power drill	4 hours' use for 1 unit.

GARDEN

Lawnmower	Cylinder type gives 3 hours' use for 1 unit. Rotary type gives 1 hour's use for 1 unit.
Hedge trimmer	2½ hours' use for 1 unit.

HOT WATER SUPPLY

Using a high performance, factory insulated cylinder, hot water for a family of four takes about 67 units per week. With timer controls, some 90 per cent of these units can be taken on the Economy 7 tariff.

Reproduced with permission of The Electricity Council.

Appendix 3
Economy 7 Tariff

Any electricity used between the hours of 00.30 and 07.30 is charged at less than half the normal rate per unit with Economy 7. These times would be from 01.30 to 08.30 during British Summer Time.

There is a very small increase in the rate per unit for the rest of the day and a negligible increase in the quarterly standing charge. Rates will, of course, vary with time and from area to area. In the following example, the rates used are those which apply to one house at the time of writing.

If the conventional tariff is used, this is what would be charged (1987):

Domestic tariff

Quarterly standing charge	£7.35
Charge per unit	5.70p

After the Economy 7 conversion, the following rates apply:

Economy 7

Quarterly standing charge	£10.15
Charge per unit	
Daytime use	6.00p
Night-time use	1.90p

The changes in the charge rates after converting to Economy 7 are:

Quarterly standing charge	up	£2.80
Charge per unit		
Daytime use	up	0.30p
Night-time use	Down	3.80p

The very large drop in the night-time rate per unit will quickly offset the increased quarterly charge and the increased day rate.

In our house we use about 1000 units of electricity a quarter. With the domestic tariff, we would pay:

Domestic tariff for 1000 units a quarter

Standing charge	£7.35
Units charged	
1000 at 5.70p each =	£57.00
Total bill	£64.35

With Economy 7, we rearrange our consumption patterns and find that half our electricity is now used at night. So the 1000 units would now cost:

Economy 7 Tariff for 1000 units a quarter with
50 per cent night-time use

Standing charge	£10.15
Units charged	
Night rate	
500 units at 1.90p =	£9.50
Day rate	
500 units at 6.00p =	£30.00
Total bill	£49.65

£64.35 — £49.65 = £14.70 saved every quarter, or £58.80 a year.

There is no charge for the conversion to Economy 7. All that is required is a new meter which is fitted free of charge.

To benefit from Economy 7 you would have to run some appliances at night. Simple, plug-in timers are now available to enable washing machines, dryers, dishwashers and so on to be run during the night.

The biggest benefits of Economy 7 will accrue to those with immersion heaters and night-storage heaters.

If you doubt whether you would benefit from Economy 7, ask your electricity showroom for a free energy survey. They will survey your premises and provide advice.

Further Reading from Kogan Page

The Blackstone Franks Good Investment Guide, David Franks, 1987

Buying and Renovating Houses for Profit, R D Buchanan and K Ludman, 1984

Easing into Retirement, Keith Hughes, 1987

Housing Grants, Nigel Hawkins, 1983

How to Buy and Renovate a Cottage, Stuart Turner, 1987

How to Cut Your Fuel Bills, Lali Makkar and Mary Ince, 1983

How to Invest Successfully, Felicity Taylor, 2nd edn, 1986

Inheritance Tax: A Practical Guide, Barry Stillerman, 1986

Living and Retiring Abroad, Michael Furnell, 1986

Personal Financial Planning, Andrew Burgess and Chris Jones, 1986

Index